CALL THEM SIOUX

Musings On Indian Cultures

In Memory of My Parents
Frank J. and Margaret Zuern

by Ted Zuern S.J.

Contents

PREFACE

The thunder storm had ended. The clouds were fragmented and allowed the sun to shine brightly in spots. As the clear sunlight passed through some still falling rain drops, it was refracted into a brilliant spectrum of colors. Subtle colors are revealed, caught between the more definite shades that give character to the bow caught in the sky.

The cultures of the world, somehow, are like that spectrum of color splashed against the sky. As pure light is shown to be composed of colors when it passes through the prism of clear rain, so the cultures of the varied peoples of earth who are united in their oneness of humanity are revealed as distinct and distinguishable entities as that humanity is thrust through the prism of creation. Humanity produces a rainbow of cultures.

The human race shares a common humanity, but that common humanity reveals a spectrum of cultures splashed around the world. Human beings with the strength and fragility, regularly associated with them, work within their group to fashion a scheme of life, a culture that is distinctively theirs. It provides nuances of meaning and understanding to the social structures of their existence, their relationships, their appreciation and interpretation of events, their grasp of life and death, their comprehension of creation, their view of their creator. Their culture will provide them with a unique, distinctive and characteristic view of life in all its ramifications. No other group of persons will have that same culture with its specific details, as does this group. They are forever united by the culture that forms them. But they will be united with all people by the humanness that all people share. They will be distinct by the culture that is only theirs, but they will still be united by their humanity with all people.

Members of other cultural groups or populations will have some grasp of what this particular cultural group recognizes in its cultural wisdom, but they will never grasp all the understanding that this culture provides for its members. It is wise to grasp as much as possible the insights and understanding that each culture provides for its members. If one should know something about all cultures of the world, he would still have only a limited grasp of the diversity of views that people possess. There are always limits to what is known. We may seek for an infinite grasp of God and his view of the universe, but it always eludes us. We are limited in our comprehension of the universe and all its ramifications. We do not possess the infinity that is proper to God. We are finite and remain so through all our searching for the wisdom that is granted to us.

Through this essay we shall look at the cultures of the American Indians, their relation to one another and to the cultures of the entire world. We shall explore the nature of culture and see what is common to all the cultures of the world and what is so distinguishing between some of the cultures of society. Cultures are composed of good and bad elements. They can move us to spiritual heights. They can reduce us to a state of degradation where we blame our culture for our lack of dignity. Because we are human and form distinct groups, we have distinct cultures with elements of greatness that enable us to grasp beyond our reach and elements of weakness that tear us down.

We shall study cultures, their unity as well as their diversity. Each culture is distinguished from all the other cultures that exist or have existed. Members of each culture will find forces that unite them as they seek to find their identity. We shall learn that we must use the culture that has been given to us. As I have had considerable experience in the Teton Lakota Sioux culture, I shall use examples from the Sioux as well as other Indian cultures. The Sioux have a culture that has had the opportunity which no other culture has had. It has entranced the imagination of the entire world. Somehow the European encounter with the Sioux shook the imagination of Europe and the world as they learned about these people whom they had found on the American plains. They were "the noble savage" of Rousseau; they were impossible to deal with when they were immediate neighbor to the Europeans and their descendants. The two had cultures that clashed. Probably no two cultures were more contradictory that those of the Europeans and the Sioux whose names for themselves is the Dakota, Nakota and Lakota peoples since they did not unite themselves under a single name comparable to the name Sioux which the Europeans called them. We shall see that the word "Sioux" was a name Europeans used in identifying them. In English those names, which are from different dialects, mean "the people", those who constitute this cultural society.

Let us look at culture, its unseen sources and influences, its relationship to other cultures, its changes, its conflicts and its place in the lives of the people to whom this culture has been given. No one ever chooses a culture; it is always given to the individual who is normally born into that culture. By the time a person is old enough to realize that cultures exist, it is too late to choose a culture for one's formation. One's formation has begun.

The Superior Self

— CHAPTER I —

In the romantic vacations lands of the world the American hotel has become almost an institution. In cities like London, Paris and Rome there are, of course, luxury hotels, but the Hiltons, the Sheratons and other recognizable American hostelries, suggesting the comfort and ease of American hotels, are scattered around the areas. They have names like the Nile Hilton that offer the notion of American convenience in an exotic location.

There is something provincial about this local, American convenience and familiarity in foreign lands. The local hostelries may reflect the way of the native people. That will include the establishments that provide high luxury of comfort to those that offer only the bare necessities of shelters. Some Americans will select either, depending on their readiness to share some experience of living in that area. But, many who can afford luxury hotels but do not have familiarity with Paris or Cairo will decide on a familiar American name. They trust that name and will expect typical American comfort when they arrive.

They know what they want and they will pay for it. As has been remarked, "I like to see foreign lands when I know that Conrad Hilton has gone ahead." There is a reserve about meeting foreign countries through a total immersion into their customs. There is bit of fear here like looking at this land through glass as one would do in a museum. On the other side of the glass may be authentic artifacts from romantic places, but the feeling of security knowing your feet are on an American floor is so desirable. It has a feeling of home while venturing into the attractive but foreign lands of the world.

In this age when American service men are stationed in varied, foreign lands, another custom is to refer to the native people by some derogatory name that spreads through all the branches of the service. "Gooks" is distinctive enough to separate the local people from the Americans. Their help is appreciated but it is the help of an inferior person. "What can you expect? They're gooks." The term became used even in America because people accept natives as inferior.

In this country Taos is a center for Western and Indian art. Pueblos which reach back before Europeans came to this country, are still used and are visited by tourists daily. I once overheard an eastern woman saying, "I don't dig this pueblo stuff. Who wants to look at a bunch of Indians living in old places? Why do they want to stay in those mud huts anyway? Why don't they get out and live like other people." Even in America there is a fear of that which is different. "Indians are not really like us." The fact that Indians settled here first, more than 20,000 years ago, does not suggest that we settlers might adjust to their way of life.

An American Westerner will say, "Don't tell me about Indians. I know all about Indians. I've live around 'em for years. They're no damn good." In contrast another person who has lived and worked with them for years will say, "They are really fine people." It may be that having "worked with them" for years makes the difference in understanding.

General Phil Sheridan's famous remark that "the only good Indian is a dead Indian" remains a part of our history, although he fought the Indian wars more than a century ago and saw Indians from a prejudicial viewpoint. It remains. It colors our view of Indians here at home.

A news account of a few years ago reported that cowboys at the Denver livestock show looked around and were uncomfortable seeing youths with long hair looking around the exhibits. They went out, grabbed a long-haired youth and trimmed his hair with sheep shears.

The iconoclast George Bernard Shaw wrote with perception, "Ignorance, ignorance, ignorance, everywhere; that is what is wrong with us, and what defeats our good intentions every time.

"What we need is not verbal wisdom; for we are stuffed with it, but knowledge of <u>the world we are living in.</u>"

We teach our children that America is the greatest country in the world and never really define what we mean by greatest - greatest in spirituality?, greatest in racial harmony?, greatest in contentment?, greatest in intellectual achievements?, greatest in law abiding citizens and communities?, greatest in honesty?, greatest in the avoidance of violence and murder?, greatest in the equal distribution of wealth?, greatest in technology with the brightest, fastest and most efficient progress for the benefit of all?

Such teaching breeds arrogance. And, arrogance closes the mind and feeds on ignorance. A definition of what we mean by "greatest"' is needed. What kind of "greatest" exists in this land? We can not blindly pre-judge; we can not pre-assess.

We as a people have such pride in our scientific method. We look at our sense of freedom combined with a scientific search for the truth. We travel because it is broadening. It is good for us to have a wider view of the world. But, often we do not really leave the narrow confines of our minds. We are shocked at the crime and murder in our streets, but we do not look at what is causing that crime and murder. Obviously with drugs in such wide use and abuse we assign such violent actions to the abusive use of drugs, but we seldom look at the roots of those actions. Those intangible roots that are invisible, that are beyond the grasp of our senses.

We have some material goals that we seek. We live in a land where so many have become millionaires that we consider that our goal. If we are not actually a millionaire, we shall buy the things we need to make others think we are. The poor "gooks" must be inferior because they have no chance of being millionaires. The Indians are another breed. They just do not understand what this world is all about although they have lived in this country for more than twenty thousand years — forty times longer than the five hundred years that our ancestors have lived here. What makes us so different when we are so much alike?

Cultural Conflict

— CHAPTER II —

I recall a meeting in Rapid City, South Dakota thirty years ago. We were a group of American Indians and two non-Indians, a radio reporter and myself, discussing how to employ for the benefit of Indians the provisions of the 1964 Economic Opportunity Act which had been recently enacted into law. For a time we discussed the issue and considered suggestions that were made. Then we sat, drinking coffee and conversing in the warmth of traditional Indian hospitality. Some freshly baked cake was served. We shared a convivial spirit and talked of various concerns. When a lull in the conversation occurred, Elizabeth Fast Horse looked at me and in a soft, matronly manner spoke the thought that was in her mind. "Father" she said, "do you know what was the worst thing you white people brought us?"

I thought a minute and tried to decide whether it might be a alcohol or tuberculosis. Before I could answer, she said, "The worst thing you brought us was money."

In the last days of the twentieth century, when money was the focus of almost every aspiration and hope, she said that money was the worst thing that white people had brought to the American Indians. In an age when judgments of persons, projects, places, property are made ultimately on the basis of money values, she had calmly said that money was the worst thing white people had brought to the American Indians!

Could she mean that? A simple reflection reveals that most Americans, probably more than they realize, tend to judge on the basis of money. Directly or indirectly, the questions they ask in trying to reach a conclusion about someone are regularly based on income, expenses and monetary values. The questions asked so regularly they are assumed to be natural, fundamental to all judgments. The questions are: How much does he make? What does he do? Where do they live? Who are their friends? What kind of car does he drive? Where does she buy her clothes? Have you seen the furniture in their home?

Calmly she had said that the worst thing was money!

The statement was contrary to contemporary culture. The statement conflicted with the accepted values of society. The statement was a contradiction.

But, the statement was a revelation of an insight. She was not talking about Americans. She was talking about Indians. To the Indians money was the worst thing that had been brought. Elizabeth Fast Horse, a Lakota woman more than sixty years of age, saw more clearly and deeply than her non-Indian contemporaries where the conflict arose between the traditional culture of the Lakotas and the cultures that had filtered out of Europe.

While there were hardships in the traditional Lakota life, money had never been a problem. Generosity was a prime value. One could not be a member of the Lakota tribe without the virtue of generosity. Generosity was used in place of money. Suppose it was already dark and a couple of visitors came to your tipi. You had absolutely nothing to serve. The only thing you could do was to see your neighbor (who was undoubtedly related to you) and ask for something to feed your guests. The honor of the tribe was at stake!

One could never allow it to be said that a Lakota tribe had received guests and not fed them. One did not need moneys. The generosity of tribal members would provide the food. Generosity was better than money. The Lakotas enjoyed a free economy. They did not have money. They did not need money. They were generous. And generosity was better than money.

This Indian grandmother who had limited opportunities for formal education grasped from her experiences and understanding of both the traditional ways of her people and the engulfing ways of European descended Americans who had come to dominate this old Indian world. She appreciated the point of difference. She recognized the cause of the conflicts in culture. She knew what many modern Americans do not know, that people could live well without money. She knew that a cultural tradition without money was possible. She knew that her people had lived very well without ever a thought of money. She knew that there were ways of life that had no need of money. She grasped the hard fact that cultures differ, sometimes contradict and frequently clash with each other.

The failure of Americans of the dominant culture to recognize the cause of conflicts in cultures was exemplified on a national scale about ten years earlier when the Secretary of Agriculture discarded his prepared speech and spoke on the absolute need for profit in agricultural production when he saw a placard denouncing the rising cost of food carried by a demonstrator. The placard read: "Food is for People — not Profit!"

In making that speech the Secretary revealed his firm grasp on an understanding of the dominant culture of this country, but he revealed the limitations of his understanding of the variety and validity of the different cultural heritages of the social groupings in the human family. He was unable, as I had been, to appreciate the existence of a culture without a monetary economy. Elizabeth Fast Horse, however, knew that at one time in this country her people, the Lakota people, had lived in a free economy. They had lived in that economy with strength and happiness. They had been the masters of the wide sweeping plains around them.

Curiously then, money which is regularly used today as the criteria for judgment is something that people have brought into existence. They have designated a material to serve as a medium of exchange. In effect they have created a factor for their economic development which in turn gives them a prime standard for judging the worth of their fellows and their actions. It is not a question of moral actions that they consider. They considered the material worth of those actions as the prime criteria of their entire worth. It is the way of one cultural group, a society that places high importance on the individual's gathering money so that he can maintain an independence from his fellows, so that he can escape community involvement that would require his physically assisting others, who in turn would assist him. It is the way of a cultural group that believes food is for profit before it can be for people.

The problem of conflicts between cultures rises from ideals that each culture provide for its members. The ideal becomes a continually sought goal for member of that cultural group. They accept the ideal as the norm and natural objective in society not only for themselves but for all other people. When they encounter members of other cultural groups who are motivated by an ideal that is different or contradictory to that ideal, there is conflict — cultural conflict.

Sometimes there is a bewildering conflict because the differences are not in something openly evident and easily sensed but in the clash of motivation from an intangible ideal that is not often brought out and examined or considered. Cultural conflict erupts, conflict rooted at the level of intangibles.

Probably there have been very few occasions when there were greater differences between members of two cultures than when the Europeans encountered the American Indians. The Europeans saw the vast acreage of America, decided that it was not really occupied and settled on this continent. At the same time the Indians believed that this portion of the earth was theirs to use. This vast land had been given to them for their use. The very thought of actually owning land was totally foreign to them. No one could own the land which the Creator had given to them for their use. It was their's to use as long as they lived. Obviously, one of the immediate points of difference was in the ownership and use of the vast continent of sweeping prairies, high mountains and rolling coast lands.

Europeans came to North America and found that they could mark out parcels of land for private use without any serious objections from the native population. Indians were helpful. In fact, without the Indians many would not have survived the first winter in this land.

Had the Indians crossed the Atlantic, discovered Europe for themselves and explored the land they found there, the situation would have been quite the reverse. They would not have been able to raise a tipi or a long house anywhere without being on the property of a private person, a corporation or a government. They would have been bewildered to find that people there wanted to stay located in one place and had permanent ownership of legally described parcels of land, real estate. They would have found themselves in a situation incredibly different from that in which the immigrants from Europe to their country found themselves. The cultural differences between them and the Europeans would have become conflicting differences far more troubling than happened in North America.

In one culture land was to be owned by individuals or groups; in the other culture land was to be used under the proper authority by anyone who needed it at a given time. The European who was formed by the ideals of his country would not give serious thought to a culture in which individuals and groups did not seek and demand title to each parcel of land. The American Indians, especially those who had grown to maturity in the northern part of what became the United States, had been formed to be casually nomadic. According to the ideals of his culture, he could not imagine any person restricting himself or his group to reside firmly and continually on a specific, limited piece of land.

When there is so much land everywhere, what reason exists for restricting oneself or group to a single parcel? The reasoning of the American Indians was sound. Given their situation in which there was so much land for relatively few people who had a nomadic inclination, the establishment of legal ownership of land was not reasonable. Furthermore, when one considers that the land produced wild fruit and supported herds of wild life, hunted and used to feed the people, one could see that this was a gift from the Great Mystery of life, God, Wakan Tanka as he is called by Elizabeth Fast Horse's people, the Lakotas of South Dakota. A decidedly sacred element has been introduced into the reasoning on the ownership of land. Can anyone truly own what actually belongs to God? Moreover, given the changes of the earth that the millennia bring, the rising of mountains, the draining of inland seas, the erosion of wind and water at all times, who does own the land on which we live, sitting as it does on solid mass covering a molten mass that circles the sun.

The initial point of conflict clearly existed when the Europeans began to settle in North America, but the point of cultural conflict was not evident to the American Indians nor to the Europeans because each assumed that the other looked on the ownership and use of land from the same cultural point of view that they had. The land was abundantly evident. The cultural concept of the position of land in each social group, the Indians and the Europeans, was absolutely intangible. Neither group could seriously consider that the other group was motivated by the cultural ideal that did in fact motivate them. The intangibles of culture were far more powerful and directive in each cultural group than could be imagined by the other group.

The Europeans directed by the ideals of their culture and recognizing that they had made the voyage to a foreign land believed that they had something to offer the American Indians. They had no regard for the Indian's culture. They had no grasp on the importance of culture in the lives of groups of people. Nor did the Indians grasp the importance of culture in the lives of the groups who had migrated to this land from Europe. The Europeans believed that they could help the Indians most by making them like themselves. They had some slight technical superiority. They had build the ships in which they sailed to this land. That, however, did not make them wiser than the Indians.

The very term "savage" which was used by Europeans in describing the American Indians indicates the attitudes and assumptions of superiority with which the Europeans came. It was originally a term that urban residents used to describe those who dwelt in the forests. It had a connotation of crudeness, a certain wildness about it. In fact, it was sometimes used in the phrase "savage beasts." The term was incredibly inaccurate.

Many basic values of American Indian cultures met and complemented fundamental values of the European cultures. Only ignorance of this common bond explains the inaccurate use of the word "savage" to describe the native Americans. The European did not realize the error he was making. Moreover, the Indians, who looked on the settlers surrounding them as people with the same background that they possessed, the same ambitions, the same expectations, would not believe that the Europeans were actually in error. The settlers were determined to develop and settle the land. The Indians never wanted to settle on developed land. They wanted to be free to move when the spirit was upon them. They could not be bound to one parcel of land for life. They shared the joys of hunting and the skills of the frontier. They even dressed alike in rugged leather when they ran out of cloth for clothing.

Later the tragic price of this error would be paid. Both sides would pay; one in blood, pain, loss and death, the other in the sense of guilt for the force and war which they and their predecessors used against the Indians.

The power of the intangible ideal is not limited to conflict between cultures from different continents. The cultural groups of American Indians as well as Europeans were wide and varied. The term American Indians is as generic as the term European. These terms specify individuals of definite continental origin but do not touch on their distinguishing characteristics. There are Swedish and Spanish just as there are Seminoles and Senecas, people of one continent but of separate cultural groups.

Among the native communities of North America there were relationships of friendship and enmity. A clear example of the latter is found in the word "Sioux" which is a corruption of the French from the Ojibway word that signified "enemy". It has the meaning of "snake". They were neighbors. They had contact with each other. Sometimes there were bloody battles.

However, another corruption by the French of the Cree word for enemy was the word, "Chippewa" for the neighbor who called themselves Ojibway. As with the word "Sioux", it was used for a vast number of people. According to the latest United States Census among the largest tribes in the United States are the Sioux and the Chippewa. Centuries have passed since they first encountered white settlers from Europe, and received the name by which they are popularly known. The misnomer is firmly fixed in the American language.

Wisdom like generosity was a highly valued virtue of the Lakota people. As one grew older, one grew in wisdom. How unbecoming was an older person who had not some touch with wisdom! An older person was respected and consulted about what one should do in any given circumstance. Generously the older person would ponder the problem and give an answer. Wisdom was important.

Europeans did not regard the distinctions that existed among American Indians. Even today, probably, the failure of most non-Indians is to believe somehow that all Indians are the same. They are not. Each tribe is different. While there are certain qualities of the Indians, such as generosity and wisdom, that are to be found in all tribes, their culture is organized in a different way.

What superiority did the technical skill of building a ship give the Europeans over the Indians? To the south in what is now Latin America the Mayan Indians had already made one of the major discoveries that the human race would ever make. The Europeans never made this discovery. The Mayans and the Arabs of North Africa, separately from each other, both discovered the use of the decimal point. They had discovered the pattern of counting in units of ten and marking the whole number from the fractions that followed with a decimal point. Without this discovery we would not have the use of modern calculators where in a flash of electronic movement we receive the mathematical answer we could seek, but only with the use of thought and time. Imagine trying to add with Roman Numerals on a modern calculator.

Of course, the genius of discovering the use of the decimal point has more to do with the ease of using figures than making possible the use of modern calculators. It is so taken for granted today that we never think of the Mayans or the Arabs who made this discovery. The discussion of superiority of cultures fades as we considered that Europeans never found the use of the decimal point. Mayan Indians and Arabs did.

Limitations of Culture

— CHAPTER III —

Memorial at Wounded Knee Mass Grave

As happens during wars, a member of one tribe would be captured by an enemy tribe. Sometimes the captive was a young person, often a mere child. Then the child would be reared by the tribe that had captured him or her and reared according to the ideals of the tribe that had captured him, not those of the child's original culture. There was no question of cultural choice. The capturers without a thought would look to their traditions for the formation of the captured child. This happened whether the child was an Ojibway or a Lakota. The cultural ideals of the captive child were not considered.

One might ask, "How could they really be considered?" Cultures are given to us. They are taught by the elders in a community. Whether Ojibway or Lakota or any other tribe, they had been formed by their elders. And, they were capable only of passing on the culture that they had inherited.

Sometimes there were not deep divisions between the cultures of alien tribes, but there was always a difference. The term American Indian must be used only in the widest and most generic sense. There is no American Indian culture. Cultures are developed by distinct tribes. The tribal members in turn were motivated by the intangible ideals of that culture.

Tragically the failure to understand the characteristics of an alien cultures can cause fear and uncertainty in persons who witness the behavior of other societies. An obvious instance of this can be seen in the bloody massacre of the Teton Lakota and the Miniconjous (both of whom were erroneously named the Sioux) by the United States Seventh Cavalry at Wounded Knee, South Dakota on December 29, 1890. The Cavalry was wary and uncertain of Indians, even in late December. They were afraid they would be massacred as in 1876 when they had been overwhelmed by the Lakotas and Cheyennes.

The last great battle between the Lakotas and the Minniconjous allied against the United States Seventh Cavalry had been fought June 25, 1876 at the Little Big Horn River in Montana. For years the name of that battlefield was named "The Custer Battlefield" in honor of the man who lost that battle. Although he and all his men were killed that day, the Indians who had won the battle but were not citizens of this country were not considered when naming the field of combat.

More than a century later, in the early 1990s, Congress passed legislation that effectively changed the name from the Custer Battlefield to The Little Big Horn Battlefield, the location of the battle.

The Lakotas fought with their allies, the Cheyenne, that day. They had left the reservation six months earlier because the Federal Government had resorted to holding back the rations promised them. Custer and the Seventh Cavalry had set out to drive them back to their reservations. He welcomed this opportunity for military action because, as it is reported, he looked on it as part of his campaign for the White House. He hoped to top off a remarkable Civil War career with a dashing routing of the plains Indians. He had, however, a very poor intelligence report. Possibly, more Indians were gathered to meet him at the Little Big Horn River than had ever gathered for battle until then. Nothing awaited them on the reservations. They won the battle and moved slowly southward to the Big Horn Mountains of Wyoming.

It had been a stunning victory for the Indians who opposed Custer. The First Centennial of the signing of the Declaration of Independence was only nine days away, July 4, 1876. Since communication from Montana to the eastern regions of the United States was without the modern means of technology, word reached people in the east only as the festivities of the century were about to begin. In effect, the candles were blown out on the nation's centennial birthday cake.

If we consider the spectacular celebration on the second centennial of the signing of the Declaration of Independence, we have some idea of what a blow the Battle at the Little Big Horn had on the nation. In 1876 all that America stood for was held high for honoring. Now some honorable people, native people, of course, who were not even citizens of this country, had somehow ruined that celebration.

However, if we will only look at the foundation in which this nation is rooted, we should not be surprised. This country was founded for a very limited group of people. It did not take in all men. It was founded for white Europeans who were escaping the restraints placed upon them by the kings and emperors of Europe.

This land was not established for the American Indians. It was not established for the Blacks nor the Orientals either. It was only for those who fled Europe.

Although a century had passed since this nation was established, no serious effort had been made to confer on American Indians the citizenship of this nation. A decade latter the Dawes Allotment Act was passed, providing citizenship for Indians who in effect would renounce their membership in tribes and struggle to be proper citizens of the United States of America.

The Blacks, incidentally, had been granted citizenship by the Fourteenth Amendment to the constitution of the United States, but so many years were to pass as States' laws were challenged in the courts of this nation giving the right to vote to the Blacks. Poll tax laws, property ownership laws, all the laws that could be imagined which were passed by states as obstacles to the rights of full citizenship were passed by states and had to be beaten down in the courts. As America was coming upon the threat of the Yellow Peril, the Orientals were far from being welcomed in this land although they would come.

The words of the Declaration of Independence, "We hold

these truths to be self-evident, that all men are created equal, that they are endowed by their Creator with certain unalienable Rights, that among these are Life, Liberty and the Pursuit of Happiness," speak of all — men. In this age of inclusive language we can recognize that word to include all women and children everywhere. But, the harsh truth is that the majority of the world's population were ruled out as possible citizens of the nation with such high ideals. Somehow, cultural differences were so deep, and rooted in such intangible ideals that it "just didn't seem proper" to extend such citizenship to all who might come.

The Indians had been here for more than twenty thousand years before Columbus landed on these shores. They had signed solemn treaties with the colonizers of this land. The responsibilities of those treaties were assumed by the United States when it came into existence. However, they were never granted the citizenship of the United States of America. Benjamin Franklin, Thomas Jefferson also George Washington and others of the founding fathers of the United States had a great interest in the Indians who lived here. The fact is that from the members of the Iroquois Confederacy Franklin learned the technique that was required to establish a government of thirteen states with the protection they need as individual states and yet have the flexibility to unite as one in facing the nations of the world. From the governments of Europe they learned only how to conquer nations and rule all as though one nation. As a nation we have much to learn about the Iroquois Confederacy and its influence on our constitution.

Of course, there were more battles. United States forces were arrayed against the varied Indian tribes who were being isolated on a variety of Indian reservations. Anguish grew among the tribal members as their cultural traditions were stultified and restrained on those reservations. The frustration of living in circumstances that restricted the response to their cultural ideals burdened Lakota hearts. There had to be some relief from such deep pain of soul!

The relief came in the form of a dance. A dance in the traditions of tribal culture is not surprising, even a dance that is a prayer if we know that culture. This dance was a liturgical response of a community imploring the Great Mystery, Wakan Takan, God. Among the members of the white community of that day dance was not considered a proper means of imploring the God of creation for relief of cultural restraints. Probably, few, if any, persons attending Church services at that time ever thought of Indians as participants in liturgical worship. But, they were. The Puritanical tradition that had remained in this land since its founding was a decisive factor in all that referred to religion. The Indians' creative imagination made them marvelous liturgists. Indians were not limited by church walls or temple barriers. They used the wide expanses of prairie, the shores of running water, refreshing mountain heights as their altars, their places of worship. The Lakotas used the stark and spectacular Bad Lands as the site for their petitioning worship. Around the world at that time there were a wide variety of tribal people who danced as part of their liturgy when worshiping God.

The summer of 1890 beheld the Lakotas dancing the Ghost Dance across the Dakotas. Other tribes in the west were also dancing. The white settlers were very uneasy. They did not understand Indians. They had even less understanding of dancing Indians. The influences of Puritanical thought was strong among them, and the connection of dancing with a religious ceremony was further evidence of the savagery of Indians. That the Indians danced a Ghost Dance, a Spirit Dance, a dance with religious implications did not give any ease to the white settlers.

They were culturally secure in recognizing that during the summer all were to work hard. Winter would come when there would not be long hours of daylight for work. But instead of working the Indians were dancing in the Bad Lands, areas of land that could well have been eroded portions of the moon, the land that had underlain an inland sea which had washed away allowing both rain and wind to erode the exposed land. In the following century when roads were built across this land, dinosaur bones would be unearthed with amazing regularity. They would be used to hold open door of gathering places and not be regarded as elements of the past. The Ghost Dance had been introduced by Wovoka, a Paiute Indian of Nevada. His English name was Jack Wilson. As Wovoka he spoke to all who would listen. He had received a revelation for the deliverance of the Indians from the oppressive reservation life and for the return of the slaughtered herds of buffalo now in 1890 almost extinct on the range. Marvelously they would be reunited with their ancestors who had died. The white people would disappear from their land. The good days would return again. He did not preach an uprising against the whites. He asked for peace in their lives. He announced the Ghost Dance; he encouraged the Messiah Cult in which all Indians who danced would be rewarded by these blessed promises of glorious Indian life. He assured all his listeners that if they danced, the white settlers would be removed from their land. Their world would be an Indian world again as it was before the white man came and brought about such diversified changes.

Dance! Dance! Dance!

The Ghost Dance was the central ritual of the Messiah Cult. In a broad sweep from the Northern plains to the Southwest, Indians danced under the sky in groups that formed large circles of continuous movement. Some Lakotas had gone to learn about the Ghost Dance. It was actually a message compounded of Indian ritual and Christian practices, which promised the Indians a renewal of all the earth if they would live in peace, practice steady industrial habits and perform a Ghost Dance, a Spirit Dance, which God had taught to Wavoka. In March of 1890 visitors to Wovoka returned and aroused their fellows with the marvelous words of Wovoka. Maybe, the dancing would have passed, but the summer of 1890 was a disaster as far as agriculture was concerned. Rations had not arrived on time. National politics had not been reformed, so the tradition "to the victor belonged the spoils" was the result of every election and that included offices on Indian Reservations. Superintendents on the reservations had been replaced by Republicans who had won the last election. They hardly had time to adjust to office when the Chiefs Sitting Bull of Standing Rock, Red Cloud of Pine Ridge, Hump and Big Foot at Cheyenne River and other tribes collectively known as the Teton Sioux saw the hope of an opportunity to strike a blow against the Federal Government. The enthusiasm of the people gave them hope of bringing about a change.

Military troops were brought in close to the reservations. Newsmen flocked to see the Ghost Dance and send back reports about the dancing Indians who would dance until exhausted and then rise to tell of revelations they had received. Among the Lakota a warrior announced that he had seen how to make Ghost shirts that were endowed by a magical power that would make them impenetrable to bullets. The peaceful dance was no longer so peaceful. The dancing continued through Autumn of that year. In early December Fr. John Jutz, S.J., who had founded Holy Rosary Mission at Pine Ridge, South Dakota, went to the Stronghold in the Bad Lands, a broad plateau with steep sides rising from the rocks below and joined to the main body of land by a long, narrow walk way. There the Lakota danced their ritualistic rites. He went to talk with the chiefs. Only two years ago he had come to establish the mission, yet in that short time he had become well received and could meet with the chiefs and talk all night with the Oglala Lakota Indians. He had urged the dancers to return with him to the town of Pine Ridge. As dawn was breaking over the Bad Lands, one of the chiefs announced that he would return with Fr. Jutz. Others made similar announcements. Then he left with the Lakotas following him. He seemed to have done his part in preventing an outbreak of war.

However, to the north at the Standing Rock Agency orders were received to arrest Sitting Bull, a holy man of the tribe gifted with a charisma that inspired trust in his fellow Indians. He was a man of influence. On December fifteenth Indian police came to arrest him. Sitting Bull refused to be arrested. Shots were fired. Sitting Bull died.

South of the Standing Rock Reservation is the Cheyenne River Reservation where the Minneconjou Tribe of the Lakotas live. Chief Big Foot and 400 followers, men, women and children, fled their reservation in panic to seek the aid of Chief Red Cloud on the Pine Ridge Reservation. When it became known that Chief Big Foot and his followers had left their reservation without authorization of the Federal Government and were moving southward, new fears arose in government leaders and the public at large. Cultural differences had left both the settlers and the Indians uneasy. Untrusted parties of the opposition were making moves that made each side insecure as they looked around them.

Of course, when the Minniconjou Lakotas came to the vast Bad Lands, they found no Oglala Lakotas. They trudged south toward Pine Ridge where they hoped to find Red Cloud. On December 28, 1890 they were captured around dusk by the Seventh Cavalry of the United States army and taken to their camp at Wounded Knee. When morning broke on December 29, 1890 the Indians were searched for any weapons they might have. Tension was high on both sides. Neither trusted the other. Each feared any action the other might make. Suddenly a gun was fired and an instant massacre was under way. The soldiers lost 25 to gun fire. The Minneconjous lost more than 200 men, women and children. The exact number is not known since the Lakotas buried some of their dead who had been taken from the battlefield. Nor is there any firm knowledge of who fired that fatal shot. Investigations have not revealed whose gun was fired.

This is an account woven with threads of imagination and richness, of fear and military duress, of deep human distrust and anguish of soul. Impossible hopes were mingled with unbelievable dread of what the other side might do. It was an incredible clash of the intangibles of cultures. The bloody bodies of the dead were scattered along draws and gullies as the harsh winds of winter began blowing steadily southward. It was to become bitterly cold.

The Lakotas had danced a prayer in the cultural tradition of their society. Those who were not Indian did not understand. They had become fearful of that incessant dancing in the Bad Lands. The military acted to control what they did not understand. The tragedy of Wounded Knee drifts forever in our national memory and the tribal memory of the Lakotas. One member of the tribe has said to me that she never drives down that road to Wounded Knee without thinking of what happened there. It is an instance in which cultural conflicts burst from the level of intangible ideals to the level of shattered bodies, lost hope and the cutting wail of the bereaved.

Somehow these calvary men, formed in the American cultural tradition which flowed from the cultures of Europe, were not able to pause after this massacre and determine what had gone wrong. They had been possessed by fear and reacted under the threat of fear, just as the Minniconjou warriors had reacted. The Seventh Cavalry had superior weapons and easily won the victory. They would be recognized as the soldiers on the hill at Wounded Knee. The nation recognized them as heroes. The Congressional Medal of Honor, the nation's highest award for military heroism, controlled action in the face of mortal danger, was awarded to more than a dozen soldiers of The Seventh Cavalry.

When members of different cultural groups clash without any understanding of what motivated the other group, wrong decisions, wrong actions, wrong recognitions follow. So frequently it is misinterpreted as the strange behavior of those people.

The Lakotas had been looking for a way to the long ago. The settlers, on the other hand, could not imagine how desperately the Indians were searching into the depths of their lives for that intangible ideal that would lead them from the virtual imprisonment of the reservation.

The triumphant experience of the Little Big Horn where sheer numbers of warriors out-matched Custer's cavalry had happened only fourteen years before. Then came the humiliating experience of the reservations which brought about the Messiah Cult when in desperation they looked to a mystical way of surviving. Then the slaughter of the Minniconjou refugees who were seeking aid from Red Cloud at Pine Ridge. This was the great cultural clash between the Europeans and their descendants with the native people whom they called the Sioux.

Limits of Culture

— CHAPTER IV —

A trained observer can always recognize an argument in a disagreement that is based on cultural divisions. The logic that the individual uses to support his statement, curiously, is never based on the structured reasoning that would explain his position. While this might be expected to be found between members of different cultural groups, it is also found among subdivisions within a cultural group.

These subdivisions arise from geographic locations, economic status, religious and philosophic commitments and other sources. When a controversy arises, the reasoning given for a position begins by making appeals to an authority of a tradition. Since the opposite side does not recognize the authority and tradition, the next appeal will be with statements like: "Where I come from, we always do it this way!", "I have never heard of people doing that!", "I was always taught to act this way!"

The appeal is always to a cultural tradition that is accepted by the cultural group to which the defender belongs. The shock of considering a contradictory cultural pattern, assumption or attitude is expressed by the complete denial of the opposing side. The two are motivated in their actions by intangible values of their cultures.

This observation is not made to indicate an error in argument. The statement, "We never do that where I come from!" is not erroneous. It is a statement of fact. It is a reflection of the cultural tradition of the speaker. Members of some cultures never dance a Ghost Dance or any other ritualistic dance as a part of their liturgies. They are honest in recognizing that in their tradition there are no ritualistic dances. However, they will become more liberated and broadened in their outlook when they can recognize that members of some cultures do perform such dances and do not become less human because of it.

In this light it is of interest to note that today when the collapse of the Soviet Union is a reality, the parts of that union have sought recognition as smaller individual states. The protection that Stalin sought for Communism has withered completely. The smaller states of eastern Europe feel more themselves in their own cultural, national states that were forced to support Communism in its movement toward One World.

In Great Britain there are movements toward a separation of Scotland and Wales. Spain has the Basque movement for independence as well as the Catalonian movement for autonomy. Germany has been united again but no one will mistake Munich for Hamburg. The cultural differences are too great. In France Normandy is not only geographically but also culturally far removed from Provence. In Italy the culture of Lombardy differs from that of Calabira, and Switzerland has in its mountainous cantons cultures that are German, French and Italian. Probably there are more subdivisions than we can imagine.

Could it be that the human way of establishing a union of states within Europe is not by uniting the members of the common market, but by uniting Scotland and Normandy, Wales and Hamburg, the English and the Basques, Bavaria and Catalonia, the individual cantons of Switzerland and all the other sub-divisions of European Nations? Rather than uniting the nations composed of varied cultures, let us consider uniting the cultural groups that form the varied schemes of living that make up Europe. This is merely a reflection based on the existence of cultural groups. Could some benefit come to each of them if there were a union of all of them? England and France, Germany and Italy and all the European nations would become less significant and the individual cultural societies within each of them would be more important.

Remember the Iroquois Confederacy? The Indians were able to contribute significantly to the organization of the United States by their tolerance of distinct units or states. They saw that each distinct state was recognized and had rights that must be preserved while the United States would deal with international relations and other affairs best served by the action of the larger government.

The small units of culture that are clearly found in the national governments of Europe are not limited to that continent. Within the United States of America there are many division of culture. Often there are further sub-divisions of culture. This is not to suggest that cultures are regularly divided and sub-divided as wheat in a granary. Members of a distinct culture produce a variant of that culture as some members move to a new location or experience a sudden abundance of material wealth or a sudden loss of the same. Various factors can explain changes in cultural life.

Members of the mainstream of American culture often do not think of divisions within their culture, but can recognize differences when references are made to minority cultures. The common observation that America is a melting pot of cultures might be worth considering. The French and the Germans, the English and Italians, the Polish, the Danish, and of course the Navajos and the Mohawks and all the other cultural groups who live in the United States have lost some of their ethnic cultures but have not established an absolutely identity with every other cultural group living in this land. All have not become one. Possibly the cultures which are native to this country have changed less than those from foreign lands, but all have changed. Yet deep within each cultural group, elements of culture remain unchanged. Certainly with the passage of each generation more and more of the original culture is lost. Often one can notice these changes with the death of the matriarchal figure in a family. A complicated preparation of a food is not made by her descendants who often will remark about Grandmother's cooking.

There is a tendency to think of minority culture as monolithic as though all were tightly bound into one absolute and unchanging structure of values. Such thought is prejudiced. It has not entered into the other minority cultures. Each member of the other minority cultures is viewed not as an individual human being, but as a conditioned, unswerving follower of an unchanging pattern of life.

When during February, March and April, 1973 several hundred Indians and some non-Indians occupied Wounded Knee, South Dakota, that community again became a focus of news for the world. At that time I was a resident of the Pine Ridge Indian Reservation on which Wounded Knee is located. As I had one of the comparatively few phones on the reservation, I received calls from newsmen as far away as Sydney, Australia, from concerned citizens across the country, from government officials and from members of the hierarchy of the Church. In each case the question was, "What do the Indians want?"

In the minds of the questioners there were no concerns about complication caused by the domination of a " white government" within the Indian community on the Pine Ridge Indian Reservation. There was no recognition that a deep, severe and ugly breach, caused by the failure years ago of the dominant government to keep its many promises to the Indian tribes, now pushed Indians into hostile and antagonistic factions standing against the "federal government." There was no recognition of the fact that Indians saw the Pine Ridge community as a "we and them" community. Actually, the deepest, most bitter feelings did not flash between the Indian occupants of Wounded Knee and the non-Indians of the area, although there was hostility between those two groups. The deepest, most bitter feelings flared between the Indians who occupied Wounded Knee and the Indians who did not occupy Wounded Knee or were against that occupation. Some remained opposed to domination by the United States. Others had adjusted to the United States and were willing to function as provided in the arrangement that had been worked out. That division can be seen in the leaders of the two parities, Russell Means of the American Indian Movement and Richard Wilson, Chairman of the Oglala Sioux Tribe.

The tragedy that remains on the reservation is the bitter wound of division within the Indian community. It is a question of each group's loyalty. Until this day the effects of the occupation of Wounded Knee are felt on that reservation. It is not a question of "What do the Indians want?" It is a question of what each group wants in working out a solution to the broad as well as specific difficulties the whole community faces. Indians are as diversified as any other group now in America.

A certain comfort comes from placing the intricacies of human relations and cultural differences into categories firmly boxed into absolute divisions. Every thing is fitted into its own category without any possible overlapping into another category. With such a structure for the consideration of human relations, definite, unqualified answers can be given. However, the answers will neither reflect nor relate to the real situation. Persons make choices. Members of the same cultural group make different choices on occasion. At times the choices are in bitter conflict. The history of civil wars are records of brother fighting brother over conflicting ideals. Their commitment to opposite ideals is reflected in the bitterness they unleashed against each other.

To give an answer to the question, I suspect, we have to look at what the group which occupied Wounded Knee wanted. They were probably very close to the Ghost Dance. There was less of the mysticism that Wovoka preached in the Messiah Cult. Now they were citizens of the United States. They were familiar with the United States Supreme Court. Their hope was for justice, recognition of the commitment that the United States had made in signing treaties with the tribes.

Such a large part of population of the United States has no real grasp that as a nation they have made promises, based in solemn treaties, with the Indian tribes. Whatever the forgetfulness of records and history of the non-Indian population, the Indians remember. Among themselves they talked about the promises made to them. They have shoe boxes of papers that they review. In some instances they bring law suits to court where they win, because promises are to be kept.

As a favor to some older Indian men, I use to type the minutes of their meetings regarding treaties that the Lakota tribe

31

had signed with the federal government. They would meet privately but would bring in hand written minutes of the meeting which I would type for them. The federal government had long forgotten these treaties and had filed them away in the National Archives, but among the Indians they were a source of continued discussion. They were pondering what the government should do for them in return for the land it had received from the tribe.

Thirty years ago there were hardly twenty-five Indians who were attorneys. Today there are over two thousand Indian attorneys. They go to court. They present their case. They win.

Most recently the Catawba Tribe in South Carolina won recognition of a treaty they made with the King of Great Britain. The United States assumed responsibility for the treaty once it was established, and though it passed legislation such as the Indian Trade and Intercourse Laws, it failed to carry out their provisions. These laws prohibited the Indians from losing any of their property without their consent. This was an obligation that the federal government promise to oversee. They had lost 144,000 thousand acres. No government agency was at all concerned about this loss. But the Catawbas were concerned. They waited with patience and now, when there are Indian attorneys and some few of other races who represent Indians, they entered into an agreement with the Federal government, State of South Carolina government and the local county government. They will not receive 144,000 acres again, but they are being given some land and a financial settlement that will enable them to establish themselves more fully in today's world.

About ten years ago the Oneida Indian Tribe of New York state, brought a case to the United States Supreme Court. They, too, had lost land that the Federal Government had promised to protect. The commitment to fulfilling the details of the Indian Trade and Intercourse Laws which George Washington as President had promised to keep, were not kept after he left office. The Oneidas brought suit for the land used for highways and roads in Monroe and Oneida Counties because they did not wish to deprive anyone of their home.

After they had lost their land the Oneidas wrote a letter to every new President as he entered office asking for the opportunity to discuss their land claims with him. Not one of our Presidents ever agreed to meet with them, but they filed in the Archives of the United States the letters received from the Oneidas. Their attorney brought these letters from the National Archives as evidence in the trial. They won the case.

They had no intention of using the land on which the highways and roads of Monroe and Oneida Counties. Instead they used this victory to pressure New York state into recognizing their claims. In that they were effective. They had won a decision that they would use to reach an agreement with the federal and state governments. When the bill was introduced, hundreds of New Yorkers from Oneida and Monroe Counties came to testify before Congress. None of them truly understood the bill. Their testimony was to the effect that no one would ever take their homes. Obviously, no one wants to lose their home, but the panicky residents revealed how little they grasped of the action that had taken place. The land which the federal government had promised to protect was taken. Now compensation in money was being discussed, but they talked about their homes as though the Oneidas had never had homes there.

In the early days when Indians were not citizens of the United States of America, there was little or no hope of victory for them in the courts of the United States. That has changed now. But the present United States Supreme Court in the last decade of the twentieth century is rather hostile to Indian tribes. The court seems to have the notion that had dominated American thinking in regard to Indians when this country was founded. The Indians were not citizens and had little access to the courts. The courts must recognize the solemn promises that the United States government has made. They recognize that statement in the Constitutions of the United States in Article VI that reads: "...all Treaties made, or which shall be made, under the Authority of the United States, shall be the supreme Law of the land; and the judges in every State shall be bound thereby...."

The nation is committed to uphold the supreme law of the land. Arguments are made by non-Indian citizens that all persons in this land are created equal, and that Indians should not have any rights beyond those of immigrant citizens or their descendants. That is true, but we have to recognize the difference between citizens of original residence in this country and those who have migrated here through the centuries and their descendants.

The citizens of original residence sold their land to the government of the United States. Usually they were forced to sell under the threat of military aggression. Obviously, they placed various provisions that favored their position into the treaties when the Federal Government had no objection. These statements concerned their rights to hunt and fish and gather wild fruits on what was their land.

The rights to hunt and fish are questions that are frequently bought to court for resolution. In the state of Washington, the Boldt decision, that Indians who have treaties with the United States Government have a right to 51% of the fishing harvest of salmon and steel head trout, is a noted decision in these continuing struggles. Wisconsin river docks became the scene of rough language and violent demonstrations each spring when fish would spawn. Indians using their rights under treaties, which are the "supreme law of the land," speared fish as they swam upstream. Non-Indian citizens argued and acted violently to stop their rights to harvest fish. Such action went on for years until government action brought recognition of their rights.

In Alaska today there are suits in court seeking the right to subsistence hunting and fishing. Subsistence hunting and fishing means gather wild life and fish for the sustenance of families. The final resolution of the Alaska case has not been reached, but it is in process in the courts.

The treaties have to be observed. However, many argued that the treaties should be abolished, that we have moved into times other than those in which the treaties were signed. Treaties can only be abolished when the two nations that signed the treaties gather together and sign another treaty abolishing the original agreement. The fact that times have changed is not sufficient of itself to reject treaty agreements. We are responsible for the word of our forefathers. It is actually a question of honor. Shall we keep the word our forefathers have given?

The important thing is to recognize our fellow citizens as neighbors and friends. Many Europeans, Blacks and Asians have married into Indian tribes. What may be of interest is that the union of an Indian and an Asian gives birth to a child that has distinctly Indian features and also Asian features. This, of course, brings race into the question.

The Mongolian spot is of interest here. In most newborn babies of Indian parents there is a spot of a darker color than the rest of skin at the base of the spine. It is referred to as the Mongolian spot. In time it disappears and normally is no problem to the infant. It is a recognized phenomenon in most Asian children as well. It is a further argument for the traditional view that the Indians came originally from Asia over the Bering Sea land bridge when the earth was in a cold period and so much of the water around the north was frozen. Probably we do not give enough credit to the variety of faces and forms which rise from Asia and which are also found in American Indians.

It is interesting to reflect on Indians coming to this continent twenty-six thousand years or more years ago over the Bering Sea land bridge along with mammoths who also migrated to North America by that route. Life was hard in those days, but the people who lived then were survivors. The cultures of the world already existed. Languages were varying. Each society was in someway different from neighboring societies. When we consider Europe and Africa at that time, we have so little to grasp. No history had been written at that time. The pyramids and great structures of the world were yet to be built, but the intangibles of culture were a factor in human life.

Earlier in the twentieth century men and women of science had confidence that given a little more time, they would have all the answers to the questions about the material structure of the universe. They had the atom and saw it as the indivisible particle of material. It was absolute. All material divides into atoms. Then the atoms, instead of being beyond division, proved to have tiny structures of sub-atomic particles. The atom had parts.

The atom divides. Cultures also divide. Such divisions show up in the separation, sometimes explosive but most frequently peaceful, among the members of cultural groups.

In the history of divisions within societies there is always a melancholic place for the members of communities known as "mixed bloods", "half breeds", "breeds" or some kindred term. They are persons who have ancestry from two cultural traditions. The occasion for the union of two heritages in an individual may vary. A member of one society may have been captured by members of another society and have come to share parenthood with a member of the capturing society. Travelers, adventurers, soldiers, sailors and merchants may have lived for a long or short period in foreign communities and have become parents of a child whose primary cultural formation comes from the community of the parent who is native to that place, but the other parent has some influence in the cultural formation of that child.

In the instances of mixed cultures in the case of American Indians, the occasion was the union of tribal members with a person of European. African or Asian descent. Formerly the non-tribal member remained to live his life within or adjacent to the tribal community. Today the non-tribal member may not be so committed. The child of mixed cultural parentage, at least in earlier years, was not faced with immediate problems within the community of his birth. Usually he or she grew up with some knowledge of the cultural tradition of the non-tribal parent. As long as this was only additional knowledge and of no particular advantage over his fellow tribesmen, conflict between the two was almost unknown. However, as influences from foreign traditions became more manifest in the tribe, problems arose.

Frequently the mixed ancestry of a child on a reservation will be revealed by its surname. The name will be of non-Indian origin. The child who has both parents from the tribe will often have one of the colorful names we associate with Indians because the government ordered names to be translated into English. From that we have names like "Black Bear", "Running Fox", "Blue Thunder" or "Crazy Horse".

In the past, frequently the tribal leaders who had to deal with the white settlers and their government were often of a mixed blood generation. However, that by no means denies talent and creativity to the children of tribal parents. As we shall see, they are often talented in creative, imaginative and inspirational ways. They are the artists and craftsmen, leaders in imaginative associations, often clergymen in new churches which they founded.

Although terms such as "mixed bloods" or their tribal equivalent were used, neither the individual's blood or physical characteristics seldom caused the problem. The problem arose because the child of a cross cultural union had a dual heritage and was able to function in the tribe with a non-tribal ease that the child of only a tribal tradition did not have. He may have learned English from his English speaking parent and so could serve as a translator for agents of the United States government, traders or any other non-Indian seeking communication with a tribal member. What happened was that he had an advantage in dealing with people of American culture of European origin. The talents and abilities of the Indian child born of tribal parents in such instances was not considered.

Pressure was placed on the tribe as it suffered defeats by the United States military forces, as it suffered restrictions of boundaries on Indian reservations, as it suffered intrusions by regulations from non-tribal governments, the tribal members who had another cultural tradition found they had an advantage in dealing with those forces. The elimination of traditional ways, on the other hand, left the tribal member who had only a tradition of tribal culture with increased disadvantages. The term, "mixed blood" or its equivalent has been used, but it was not the influence of mixed blood but of mixed cultures that made the difference.

The "mixed blood" knew how to use the ways of the dominant society which was moving into the Indian world. He had an advantage. The reduction of opportunities in the traditional ways forced that advantage to become the cause of jealousies for those losing opportunities. Divisions arose. The antagonism between "mixed bloods" and "full bloods" continues on Indian reservations today. To the outside world any resident of a reservation is normally "an Indian". Yet on the reservation the "mixed blood" will often refer to the "full bloods" as "Indians" while the latter will call the former "whites". The tragedy is not

37

that appellations are used but that they are used contemptuously by brothers in the same tribe. Deprivation and the denial of opportunities are squeezed in upon the tribe. The tribes weakens; the members hurt.

Today, an almost complete reversal has taken place. With the influence of television reaching the reservations, the advantage of their native language no longer exists. Young children no longer seek to speak their language. On television everyone speaks English.

There are classes in native languages, but only those who see what has happened to their tradition take the classes. So much of cultural tradition is being lost. When one is over twenty and tries to study his native language, it is obvious that person has lost more of his culture than a knowledge of his language.

Cultural conflict is the problem not only of Indian reservations but of a shrinking world. More than at any other time in the past cultural conflict has become the concern of human persons everywhere. More members of varying cultures meet each other as the speed of travel and communication increases. The lands of Marco Polo's adventures are only hours from the land of his birth. Technical advances are remarkable; cultural understanding pains for growth. Conflict in cultures, the denial of traditional values and social structures, the opposition to beliefs and traditions are realities. Amusement is taken in ridiculing "the strange ways" of other people. Inferiority is assumed to be the characteristic of societies that are different. Human genius is overwhelming when the scientific inventions, discoveries, and accomplishments of its members is considered. But, a frustration stirs unrest in the souls of those members as they consider the failure around the earth where cultures have met only to spawn distrust and outright hate.

What is culture? What are its dynamics? Why are there such fundamental dynamics between cultures? Are some cultures truly inferior to others? Why do cultures change? Must there be only one culture for world members if peace and unity are to be a reality?

The Center of Intangibles
— CHAPTER V —

Let me relate a story that will give some insight into the hidden structure of cultures. I think it may give some insight into what should be our approach to members of other cultures.

Some thirty years ago when I was a pastor of a small church on the Rosebud Sioux Indian Reservation, a man of the Crow Indian Tribe who worked in the Land Office of the local agency observed to me that so much social damage had been caused through the years by teachers, priests, doctors, government officials and others who came to the American Indian reservations and saw the people primarily as "Indians" and only secondarily as "human beings." That approach had left Indians remote and somehow different from those outsiders who had come to the reservation. The innate humanity that American Indians share with everyone was obscured for them. They had to reach over an imaginary gap that was not there for those few who saw the humanity in all the people of world. Thus, the Indians were seen as the deprived who had to be led from their present culture to be trained to participate in the cultural ways of the outsiders.

Such an approach ignored the fact that all cultures are gifts from God. We are born into a culture and receive in it the wonders of life. In the finite human family cultural diversity reveals the infinity of our Creator. As the spectrum of colors refracted from a clear light passing through a prism reveals the variety of color within that light, so the variety of cultures reveals something about the infinity of God, the structure of society, the formation of the universe. Each culture has nuances of meaning that are different from other cultures. Only by considering the varied nuances of the world can we grasp the meaning of God, society and the universe as well as the human person.

Those outsiders overlooked the depths of tribal culture and the warmth and ease it gave to its members. The cultural distinctiveness of Indians was seen as an incipient stage in development toward the assumed prime cultural achievements of the human family. For many non-Indians the ideal of European cultures was held as an absolute standard for all cultures. Thus, they reasoned that only by achieving that ideal could American Indians become civilized and Christian. So identified with culture had religion become.

This tendency to view American Indians as somehow apart from the mainstream of the human family was revealed in much of nineteenth century American literature. Terms such as "lowly Indian" and the more condescending "pagan savage" were used regularly. Mention of civilizing the Indians indicated an incredible stance on white people toward their Indian neighbors. Furthermore, in 1879, a little more than a century ago, a United States court found for the first time that an American Indian is a human person within the meaning of U. S. law. The Indian was Standing Bear, a headman of the Ponca Tribe. The U. S. District Court in Omaha, Nebraska found "that an Indian is a 'person' within the meaning of the laws of the United States." That judicial recognition gave official and legal status to all members of native American people as human persons on a par with all Americans.

Only with considerable difficulty and reflection does the member of any cultural group extend his vision beyond the common assumptions and expectations of his own society. If society itself did not identify the Indian's human qualities, most members of that society would not do otherwise.

Intangibles are realities beyond the reach of our senses. They are neither felt nor heard, seen, tasted, or smelled. Yet if we look fully at the intangibles of life, they are the things that we are most ready to defend. They are deeply important to us. They involve our sense of honor and affection, the greatness and glory of our lives, the long enduring spirit and dedication we experience. Or on the other hand they can reach to the most base levels in our experiences. They involve words such as denial, lie, betray, ignore. Somehow, these intangibles are at the heart of our culture.

What is culture? There are many definitions of culture, but I prefer one that is descriptive of its operation. Culture is a way of living that is learned informally by children from the behavior of elders in their society.

Culture is taught. As children we receive our lesson informally from our elders. There are no formal classes in a class room. There are no lectures. We experience them and learn. Culture is a gift to us. We receive our culture. No other culture will ever have for us as individuals the warmth, the home qualities, the ease of living that we find in our native culture. Although I have traveled far and have become entranced by cultures I have seen and feel deeply within me the noble purposes those cultures express, yet I know that I can never enter any of those cultures as a child and grow with the security, the knowledge, the feeling they provide to children born into those schemes of life.

I am an American of Germanic descent born in Milwaukee, Wisconsin. I have lived most of my life in lands and states far away from that area, yet I always feel a sense of being home, a sense of my very own culture, when I return to southeastern Wisconsin. I am familiar, of course, with the Kettle Moraines in which I grew up, but it is the way of living in the Kettle Moraines by the people among whom I was born that makes me feel at home. Its intangible!

A child will accept what he repeatedly observes. He accepts the intangible cultural expectations that he observes as the unquestioned structures of behavior in the lives of those around him. The child does not reason about their value or appropriateness. He wants to do what older people do. Like a son who watches his father make repairs about the house, he will play at making the same repairs. Or a daughter will imitate her mother in performing the work of the home. In this early stage there is only the desire to act as adults in the community. No judgment is made. Elders are accepted without question; they know what is to be done when problems arise. Their actions set the pattern in the new generation of society.

Thus, the community life of a society provides the culturally accepted ways for new members of that society in meeting the problems of life. The use of these culturally accepted ways gives assurances that advancement toward the ideals of that society are being made.

Because a culture forms and shapes its own members and does not look beyond its own membership, it is distinct from other cultures. In fact, wide and extreme diversity can exist among cultures. Rather than considering such diversity a threat to one's cultural identity and a contradiction of one's cultural ideals, one should strive to see God has created humankind with a genius for fashioning with diversity the methods that societies use in meeting the challenges of life.

Normally, the more removed an observer is from the members of an alien culture, the less threat he feels from members of that culture and the more likely those member's behavior and rituals will seem quaint and romantic and "different in an interesting way." However, the closer an observer is to members of an alien culture, the more likely the behavior and rituals of those members will appear strange, if not uncivilized and barbaric. When the behavior of one culture is judged by the standards of another culture, the judgment is in error.

An analysis of culture may be made by considering culture diagramed as three concentric circles. A Center of Intangibles lies in the first circle at the very heart of the diagram. The circle represents the basic beliefs and ideals of a culture, its natural theology, philosophy of life, answers to the fundamental questions such as Who am I?, Who are other people?, Who is God?, What is the universe?, What relationships exist among us? These answers have intangible values. They exist within the minds of members of a culture. They are never seen. They are seldom questioned. They are the traditional beliefs and understanding of "my people". They are the deep, motivating forces in the lives of the cultures members. They are the roots of behavior. Like electricity, which is also unseen, they cause activity which is seen.

It may be good to observe, that God is mentioned frequently in this book. In the history of culture we have no instances of a culture without God and a practice of religion. Only with the advancement of technology does atheism appear as well as polytheism, the worship of many gods. When life is simple, men recognize one God. When life becomes complex, men deny God or worship many gods.

Atheistic communism disappeared in Russia a few years ago, and the open manifestation of religion practiced by the people of the former Soviet Union was notable. The conclusion is that while some patterns of life have been developed with atheistic qualities, no cultures have begun with them. In the course of their lives some people have become atheistic and teach that belief to their children, but there is always the recognition that other cultures recognize a God.

Because these intangibles are never seen, they are often undervalued and misunderstood by an outside observer. They are, however, the deep, motivating force within members of a culture. They exist within the minds of the members. Each member expects that his fellow members possess and use those same intangible values. In times of community crisis, when there is confusion about a particular issue, members of that society will look within themselves to examine these values and determine what they truly believe. These intangible values are the heart of a culture, but they are never seen. They are known.

Circle of Structures

— CHAPTER VI —

The second of these concentric circles is called the Circle of Structures. It surrounds the Center of Intangibles. This circle represents all the cultural structures that underlie all the social institutions within a cultural society. Through its social institutions a culture provides its members the means of meeting the basic problems of living. These means are the social arrangements for a cultural society's government, politics, worship, economics, marriage arrangements, family style, education, recreation, art, labor, management and other means of expression. The structures of society's institutions rise from the intangible value of its culture and are influenced by the circumstances of geography, climate, natural abundances or deprivations, history, native prowess, ignorance or insights and other qualities the society may possess.

Here are the accepted unwritten patterns and directives underlying interpersonal activities within a society. Whether a member is constructing a dwelling, selecting a spouse or having a spouse selected for him or her, directing a government or responding to a government directive, seeking an education, selecting food, deciding what to wear, seeking work or seeking workers, going on a journey, acting against an enemy, working to establish peace in the community or any other patterns of activity that may be needed. All that members of that society must know, so as to act properly within the traditions of that culture, are found in these unseen but known structures of its social institutions.

Cultures will usually have similar intangible values; often they are identical. However, the social institutions will normally vary. They will be different because of different influences of history and material circumstances. Each culture has a unique background that influences its cultural activity,

A psychological movement seems to operate at this level where the Center of Intangibles influences the Circle of Structures. Actions of members of the society seem to be according to the circumstances of historical and geographic location. For example, the Eskimos have made their homes of snow because it was so abundant whereas a society of jungle dwellers have selected tree branches for their homes. For clothing the American Indians of the plains used animal skins decorated with the colored feathers of birds while shepherd societies use the wool shorn from their sheep and goats. Diets of various groups depend on the availability of animals and plans available to them. There does not seem to be much reasoning for the use of resources in all these instances. The individual reaches to what is available.

An outside observer might note a certain relationship between the intangible values and the social structures of that culture's scheme of living, but that is not necessarily true in every instance. Some cultures are more aggressive that others. Some are more cunning in their ways. Women have a greater role in the government of some societies and are almost excluded from participation in others. What is an accepted mode in one culture's social institutions will sometimes be totally unacceptable in another. Thus, the behavior of one culture will be fully acceptable to its members, but will not be considered proper to another group.

It should be noted that the structures of a society's social institutions become traditional. There is little change in them, unless some event occurs to make available some other material in considerable abundance or a different appreciation of values. In defending traditions from criticism the members appeal to the custom of their people and not to the reasonableness of their actions. Here we note statements, mention above, as, "I have never heard of such an action," or "We never do that." Difference is not seen as variety in human actions but as inadequate, if not totally wrong.

Probably, in this area conflicts in culture arise because here the unseen assumptions, attitudes, approaches and expectations exist and influenced the formation of structures in the society's institutions. When distinctive structures are understood by the members of that society, there is no difficulty in appreciating why a member acts in this particular, traditional way. However, an outside observer who does not understand the expectations, approaches, assumptions and attitudes involved in this particular society can easily wonder at or condemn this mode of action. Actually the members of the culture and the outside observer may have the same goal in mind. The means that each uses will differ because of the differences in the social structures of each society.

As an example of these differences, consider the structure of government. Government could be a monarchy, a democracy, an oligarchy or various forms of representative government. Even among these types of government variations can exist. Unless an individual is disturbed by a malfunction in his government, he will normally accept it as appropriate for himself and his peers. When traditional beliefs exist within members of a given culture, fellow members do not tend to question the actions of others because they are traditional actions for that community. Those outside the community's cultural formation more easily question the appropriateness of the actions. They will have different attitudes, assumptions, approaches and expectations formed by the traditions of that culture.

A factor in this establishment of structures in a culture could well have something to do with an experience I had some ago I was the director of Red Cloud Indian School. I had years of experience with Indian students and wanted to offer the best curriculum possible. I had observed that the Indian students I knew were creative, artistic, graceful persons. Basketball, not football with its violent action, was their game. They were smooth, limber, lithe, willowy, fluid in their movements up and down the court, over the basket, shooting goals. This is not the image that those who have not taught Indians have of them, but it is only a sign of how much many have to learn about them.

If I were pushed to describe in one word, the Indian students

46

I had, it would be "poetic". They are "poetic Indians." They were great at giving nicknames to each other. They would select the one, notable quality an individual possessed and then fashion a name from or around that quality. As writers they were creative, great story tellers, an answer to a creative writing teachers dream.

For art classes one can hire an art educator or a true artist to teach its art curriculum. The art educator teaches students how to arrange in a design popcicle sticks. An artist teaches them how to paint pictures, mold ceramics, form sculptures, how to become artists. The artists who were hired at Red Cloud school often remarked how rapidly and instinctively the Indian students learned the basics of art. It was as though they had a special gift.

Reflecting on their gift as liturgist, using motion and song, literature and movement, color and design to express the feelings of the congregation, it seemed that special classes should be given them. That would satisfy the inner artistic ability they had. They would be good. Of course, one had to demand that they meet the requirements of mathematics, reading, spelling and other required subjects.

The school began in 1969 holding the annual Red Cloud Indian Art Show which is open to all Indian artists. The overwhelming success of that annual show remains a wonderful experience in my life. As a collection of art and sculpture were gathered each year, paintings were place around the school so that the students could see the creative work of their elders.

I found the emphasis placed on art, a direct affirmation of my conviction that Indians are artists. Not all of them are, but there is a greater number of them than we find in other populations groups. They are poetic.

Having accepted an assignment in Indian ministry off the reservation, I began to hear one day about the influence of the right hemisphere of the brain. I learned that according to this theory most of us are influenced by the left hemisphere and as a result are logical, mathematical, very businesslike, inclined to move from one solid conclusion to another. Those who are influenced by the right hemisphere of the brain are creative, inspirational, intuitive, able to imagine what they have not seen.

Instantly I saw some explanation here for the poetic ability of the American Indian students I had known. Not all are influenced by the right hemisphere of the brain, but a larger percentage than is found in ordinary society are so influenced. Likewise, not all members of the non-Indian American society are influenced by the left hemisphere of the brain. There are non-Indians who are artists. I do not know how deep the proof is for this theory of influence by the right and left hemispheres of the brain, but I do know that a larger percent of Indians are poets than is true in the dominant society of this country.

This is one of the intangibles that we deal with in trying to learn how culture works. It is one of the factors that takes the intangibles we never see; things like love, loyalty, dedication, a sense of honor, courage, reverence, sorrow, grief, an awareness of greatness and dignity, self-worth, humility and commitment. These intangible qualities are formed into social structures as they move onto the second circle of this cultural scheme.

The Lakota tradition of warfare is another example to consider at this level of social structures. When modern warfare is considered, pictures of massed troops and armaments come to mind. For the Lakota this was not the case. For the Lakota man, the ideal role was that of the warrior-hunter. Hunting was necessary since that was the only way to gather meat. They lived at a time when large herds of buffalo grazed the country. They would wait for the approach of a herd and, after the arrival of the horse to this land, would sweep down on the herd with bows and arrows and lances riding lightly among the herd, killing the large animals which provided hundreds of pounds of meat as well as a amazing variety of materials for the other needs of life. Women would come in after the slaughter by the warriors and begin to butcher the buffalo, cutting the meat, saving the hides and bones, sinews and internal pouches, horns and hoofs, all that could be used in the daily course of life. All the animal was used. Hides for tents and clothing and moccasins, horns for decorations, select bones for special uses, buffalo hair for stuffing pillows and a wide variety of many other uses were found in the slaughtered buffalo. I have seen a list of over 100 uses of buffalo parts. The herds of buffalo were a walking supermarket of today. Practically everything could be found in the buffalo.

Without being a warrior there was no way for a man to advance in the societies and governance of his tribe. There were individual men who did not relish this style of life and would not follow the pattern of a warriors life. The tolerance of the Sioux people became evident in these instances. They were accepted as members of the tribe, but not as warriors. They would not become leaders of the tribe. Frequently their sexual preference was not for women. They would have their own tipi and usually be noted for the excellence of their bead work and other crafts.

One of the big problems that the United States government had in its first century of existence was to stop Indian intertribal wars. One of the reasons for the signing of treaties between the Federal Government and the Indian Tribes was to have each tribe pledge a state of peace among the tribes. But how could that work when in the very culture of the tribe was the need for honoring warriors who went off in small groups to attach an enemy tribe? After each treaty was signed there would be a period of up to six months in which peace prevailed, then a group of warriors would slip off to attack another tribe. The chief of the tribe did not direct this activity and the tribe would not be responsible for it. It was the difficulty in understanding this part of the culture that kept the European settlers and their descendants so frustrated in the process of treaty signing. The very thing that gave an Indian warrior prominence in his tribe was the subject of prohibition by those of European descent who would approve the formation of armies and battles with countries who did not accept their foreign policy. Indians had difficulty in understanding the cultural distinction.

I recall an instance in the late 1960s when a Medicine man was brought from the reservation to make a young man a chief. By that time the role of chief was only a memory from the past. No one would have added any obligations to him. It was a case of his grandmother wanting him to be so recognized. So the family put on a feast and had this grandson named "Chief". A woman of that tribe was visiting with me after the event and remarked, "How can they make him a chief, he hasn't even been

49

in the army." That was recognition of the tradition of chiefs rising from the warrior societies, but since there was no warrior society now, a young man's service in the army, navy or marines was accepted as a cultural substitute.

Often it was not a large band of warriors fighting an enemy tribe, but a few young men, six or seven, slipping away to attack an enemy tribe. Quietly they would ride to the enemy camp, scout the scene and when the right instant was found, would ride directly at an enemy, touch him and escape unharmed. This was called "counting coup". For each encounter he was allowed to wear an eagle feather. The angle at which he wore the feather indicated the difficulty of his manoeuvre. If it was upright on his head, it signified that he had "counted coup" directly. If it was worn at other angles around his head, it signified an encounter of lesser difficulty. The destruction of the enemy was not the object of war except in instances when, as at the Little Big Horn, they were motivated to seek revenge. There were tribes with whom the Lakotas were on friendly terms. They would sometimes fight in alliance with these tribes against the traditional enemies.

Children would recognize how important these men were when they would return having counted coup. The whole tribe would celebrate with dances and rousing victory speeches that would go on into the night. Such celebrations would deeply impress young boys with ideals for themselves. The culture was being transferred to the next generation, but government agents could not realize why the tribes would not listen to their plans for peace. Culture was at work in the Indians.

They thrived on their limited warfare which would not be compared to the full military force of the United Sates Army. In their own culture it gave them a reason for living. It was important to them as individuals. It was important to the whole tribe.

Chiefs of Indian tribes understood the importance of their type of warfare to the tribe. Individual chiefs would not always lead an enemy attack. It might take place without his knowledge. He knew how important it was to "count coup", to add eagle feathers to a warrior's war bonnet, to celebrate a warrior's brave feats of victory and the honoring ceremonies on his return. He had a certain pressure on himself from the United States government for the failure to outlaw war. He knew his people and the cultural importance of their form of limited warfare. He could not outlaw it without betraying the culture of the tribe.

After Europeans had taught friendly Indians to scalp their hostile Indian enemies as proof of a kill for which the Europeans paid them, scalping became an accepted form of Indian warfare. When there were deaths in battle, the scalp was normally brought back and exhibited at the victory celebration. Such changes in culture took place and became a permanent part of the tradition on how to attack an enemy.

The words of an ancient author seems to have hit upon these thoughts. He wrote in the book of Ecclesiastes, a book concerned with the purpose and value of human life. In chapter 3, verse 11 he wrote about the hidden relation between man and God. He wrote, "He has made everything appropriate to its time, and has put the timeless into their hearts, without men ever discovering, from beginning to end, the work which God has done." There are intangible values in human life, and somehow men construct equally intangible social structure that define the efforts of their lives.

Circumference of Tangibles

— CHAPTER VII —

Standing Bear ©HRM

Within the third concentric circle lies the Circumference of Tangibles. Here are the visible, sensible, tangible elements of a culture. Their roots reach through the Circle of Structures down to the Center of Intangibles. Here are the behavior patterns, the customs, the social habits, the mores, fashions, styles, patterns, mannerisms, rituals, rites, practices, designs and conventional usages of materials that are exhibited by members of a culture. Here the tangible makes visible the intangibles of culture. Here the materials needed for the conservation and enjoyment of life are put to use and become traditions of individual cultures. The visible uses and employment of the materials available to a culture become part of the structures in the social institutions of that culture. Here are the designs of architecture and dress, the distinctive characteristics of a art whether they be fine arts or the performing arts, the unique customs and menus, the form of government, the method of education, the recognition of heroes and the condemnation of cowards, the qualities this society honors in its members, the goals this society seeks and all that is visibly or in some sensible way found by the human senses. Here the differences are easily perceived. A warm German cap is not confused with a Lakota headpiece of feathers. Movable tipis are easily distinguished from skyscrapers. Light tropical dress is never identified with the furs of Eskimo garb. Even the conferring of honors differ as a medal of honor is distinct from an eagle feather. The roots of tangible culture reach downward into their social institutions and down into the basic intangible values.

In contrast to the movement from the Center of Intangibles to the Circle of Structures, which has been described as psychological, the movement from the Circle of Structures to the Circumference of Tangibles seems to be a logical movement. Given the structures of social institutions and the circumstances in which the members of that culture live, there seems to be a logical use of the materials available to them.

There is a natural tendency to compare cultures on the basis of what is tangible, visible, reached by the senses. However, the deep roots of every culture are in the Center of Intangibles. The tangibles are understood only in terms of the intangibles, the fundamental values of a culture.

Sometimes there is a comparison of a dance to a dedication. When this is done, a tangible is compared to an intangible. It is a case of comparing ideals and performances. The two subjects are different in nature. The subjects being compared are not equal. There may be a relationship between them but no true comparison. One is reaching from the tangible to the intangible.

The Eskimo had an abundance of packed snow which lend itself to the construction of an enduring home, the igloo. The relatively scarce list of materials that could be used for home construction logically led to the snow which they had in abundance. In the southwest the use of adobe bricks for the construction of housing is another example of the logical use of native materials for the creation of dwellings. In our time when there is such a wide assortment of building materials, high rise apartments are very practical for providing many homes in an area of dense population.

The weaving of fabrics from cotton and wool provided a wider choice for dress. Prior to their development, leather and furs from animals, or in tropical locations, large plant leaves were the logical choice for clothing. Style and distinction in dress were a principle in the dress of the Plains Indians. They had an abundance of leather and furs. They used shells and elk teeth as well as the colored feathers of birds, dyed quills of porcupines, later replaced by glass beads brought from Europe, in designing their distinctive dress which was the most notable of all pre- Colombian clothing on the plains. Curiously, we look to women for the stylish dress with intriguing cuts and a variety of colors and accoutrements, but among the Plains Indians the men wore headpieces of regale eagle tail feathers, white with black tips, or softened porcupine quill roaches with one or two feathers rising easily above their heads and the bustles of colored feathers, yellow, green and orange with a striking slash of red, marked with distinctive ornaments outshone the women's costumes. They sensed the impressive appearance that they made and posed with striking posture in their regal regalia. Their human instinct, their sense of style, the influence of the right hemisphere of the brain guided then in fashioning extraordinary dress.

The difficulty required for finding and preparing colored feathers for their dress did not stop the Lakotas in their search for the perfect garment. The intangible sense of fascinating style that the Lakotas possessed rose from the Center of Intangibles to the Circumference of Tangibles where it was seen and admired.

Let us look at the differences in government. The Lakotas came closer to a true democracy, rule by the people, than did the European settlers who had decided on a republican form of government. We are familiar with a republican form of government since the United States uses that form of government. The Lakotas had a chief to head their government, but he was not necessarily the son of the former chief. It was not an inherited position. The council of elders, a group of older men, wise and conservative, made the selection when it was necessary to have a new chief. Of course, he had to be a warrior with a good record. He had the right to wear many eagle feathers, but there were other qualities that he had to have.

He had to be an orator. Good public speaking was always a part of a leader. While the council of elders probably never thought about it in such terms, they looked for a man with a sharp sense of psychology. He had to be a senior diplomat, capable of meeting with officials of other tribes or the United States. He needed to be a just judge, a man who could look at a case and come up with a decision that was appropriate. That did not mean all persons were equal. Women were subject to their husbands. If a wife should leave her husband without a divorce, he had the right to cut off the tip of her nose.

In debate there was no thought of time. It was necessary to hear everyone who had something to say. A council meeting could go on for days if no agreement was reached. Agreement was by a total consensus of the group. If consensus could not be reached, the proposal was not accepted. It might come up again at a later date, but all had to be able to state their opinion on the subject.

The characteristics held in highest esteem by the Lakota were wisdom, generosity, courage and reverence. From experience and from listening to his elders a man or woman should be a wise person. They should have a sense of what was to be done in handling a situation of life, the safety of the tribe and all that pertained to tribal members. He should act with a prudent manner, never rushing into some problem of which he had no knowledge but rather reflecting, quietly meeting the challenge.

The Lakota person should be generous to his neighbor. To this day many Indian men who grow up in modern society and see the frequently ungenerous way of the world will remark how as children they were taught to be generous to their fellows. Sometimes when they were experiencing the natural greed of childhood, they had no inclination to share what little treasures they had. In a quiet way their father or another elder pointed out the choice that was theirs, and indicated what a good Lakota person would do in that situation. Always it was to be generous to those in need. That remains a quality they keep. It may put them in conflict with the ways of the modern world, but it makes them a Lakota. Often as a child it was a hard decision to make, but the memory swill remained with that person all his life. As he made the decision to be generous, he accepted the Lakota quality and furthered it in his life.

Courage is a quality that was needed in the wilderness as well as in the technical world of modern life. Courage is the virtue we possess when in the face of threatened danger to ourselves we go ahead and perform a difficult act. Because of courage, we have heroes. A parent may recognize the threat to his life from a burning building if he or she thinks of entering that flaming structure to rescue a child. Dashing through the flames of fire and saving the child from certain death is a heroic action. The person who does that is a hero. The normal fear of fire would turn a person of lesser courage from such an action. The Lakota knew that and sought courageous leaders. The counting of coup in warfare, actually touching an enemy and escaping again, is another example of courage. The Lakota leader had to be comfortable with that virtue. It had to be a quality of life for the Lakota.

Reverence is the other characteristic that was looked for in a chief. He had to be a person who habitually acted with reverence and respect for others, the members of his family, of his community or tribe, even his enemies. There would be variances in his treatment of his wife and his enemy, but with both there would be a regard for the dignity of that person. It was necessary to be a leader of true dignity that allowed a show of respect and reverence for others.

The Lakota characteristics were wisdom, generosity, courage and reverence. It is interesting to note that traditionally in the thought of the Western world the moral virtues were prudence, justice, fortitude and temperance. Wisdom and prudence have a similarity.

They suggest age in a person and a thoughtful behavior. Generosity and justice indicate the giving to another what is due them or what is necessary for their survival. The person in desperate need has a claim in justice. Courage and fortitude are similar without any consideration of what they involve. Usually these characteristics summon up visions of strength brought to bear against harsh physical pressures bearing against an individual, but they can be forces of spirit girded against spiritual powers seeking to reduce this spirit to impotency. Under any circumstance firmness of will is required. A challenge has to be faced which any person would rather avoid.

Reverence and temperance have much in common. One thinks before acting and exhibits a modest deportment when one is reverent, while temperance requires one to maintain a demeanor that is sober, balanced and in accord with proper behavior. While temperance has a relationship to avoiding or moderately using alcoholic beverages, in a deeper sense in relates to all that attracts a person. It is closely related to reverence.

These characteristics or virtues are rooted in the Center of Intangibles in the Lakota and Western cultures of Europe. Again intangibles are so important in our culture, in our lives, in what is meaningful to us. The similarities between these intangibles in the two cultures which are so different on the level of tangibles indicate that possibly all cultures have the same intangibles but end up with different Circles of Structures and Circumferences of Tangibles. The structuring of social institutions are psychological in nature. At that level the individuality of the societies come into operation and prepare for the individualism of the cultures, that is the distinct, unique, individual style, pattern and scheme of the cultures.

It is interesting to note that in the traditions of the Iroquois Confederacy, in contrast to the Lakota tribes, women had a distinctive role to play in the process of government. Their way of life was a matriarchy; women possessed the home and its fixtures, all inheritance was through the mother since she and not her husband had possessed property that could be received by heirs. But, the point to be made here is that women formed a council which selected the names of men who might become chief and then submitted this list to the men's council who chose the individual for that honored role.

This age, which is so secular and dedicated to the notion that all good will come from the expanding field of technology, may find it hard to recognize that the Indians, like all our ancestors, lived in a far more sacred world than we know. Everything in their world was sacred, wakan, holy. In this regard his book "The Idea of the Holy" by Rudolf Otto has a idea for our consideration. He considers how words change their meaning with the passage of time. His concern is with the word "holy". The original meaning of "holy" was a reaction to a manifestation that left an individual in a state of astonishment, wonder, awe. The experience was beyond what normally happened in life. Gradually the word came to be used in reference to manifestations of God. The word would be used in reaction to a wondrous sunrise or a breathtaking view of a valley from a mountain height. Whatever would leave a person with a sense of awe. The original word began to spread its meaning of awe and began to be used in a related way, specifically in regard to God who would leave the imaginer with a sense of awe as he began to realize the ramification of the divinity.

The Lakota word "wakan" has this same meaning. It is now used of God, but formerly it had a meaning lesser physical manifestations. The Lakotas will speak of the world as wakan, holy. It has been given to them by God and is to be reverenced, respected, honored. It is used with "tanka" which means "great" to signify their word for God — the Great Holy One, the Great Mystery or as some say the Great Spirit. It seems best to give a variety of translations for someone so beyond human comprehension.

The world is wakan and must be used in a respectful way. It must be used with reverence, with piety. Each day began with prayer. Lakotas, men and women, would face the east as the sun rose to warm the day and offered morning prayers to their Creator who was now providing this day which they would use worthily. In the course of the day as a significant event occurred, they would again pray to Wakan Tanka for guidance in their actions. The hunter would pray to the spirit of the animal he was hunting. It was a sign of reverence, of appreciation, of gratitude for the gift of its flesh for the subsistence of his family. The qualities of reverence and gratitude are repeated throughout his life. The Lakotas had received a culture that was charged with reverence and gratitude. How that contrasts with the popular notions of Indians with so little regard for their inner feelings and sentiments!

The secular attitude of this age would be completely foreign to the traditional Lakota people. To take the gifts of this earth for granted would never enter their minds. The universe had been given to the Indians. They revered it and the One who gave it. This reverent way of behaving was a way of life for them. In some regards the early settlers from Europe had some of the same reverence, but with the changes in culture that we have experienced in this age of technology, we are far removed from that custom of respect.

The naming of relatives is important because frequently we are convinced that our way is the right way. The Lakota people used the extended family in counting relatives. The grandparents in a family were the head of the family arrangement. The grandchildren called "mother" not only their birth mother, but all her sisters. Thus it was normal for them to have many mothers. It was not a case of the mother who bore them having a position of honor. She and all her sisters were designated as mother. Likewise the father and all his brothers were called "father" by his children. Husbands and wives of the mother's sisters and the father's brothers were aunt and uncle. However, the children of the sisters and brothers of their birth parents were called sister and brother. This extended family was, obviously, much larger than the nuclear family of today. Since the family lived all its life in the same community, these brothers and sisters had continual contact with one another. With this arrangement it was possible for a child to have sisters and brothers of his own age. The daily association with these brothers and sisters built strong family bonds. Since the Lakotas did not have last names as happens in our society, there was no problem with children having different last names in that society. It was a case of from what family they were descended. In this arrangement each couple had their own tipi, but in some instances two or more families would share a tipi. One of the joys of childhood was sleeping at a brother or sister's tipi. The birth parents would not be disturbed by the child being away at night. Why should they be concerned? The child was with his or her brothers and sisters in a neighboring tipi.

Today there is so much influence from the dominant society on the Indians that the traditional way of counting relatives is less in use. However, one frequently hears a Lakota remark that they are "sister (or brothers) in the Indian way" which means that they are cousins as relatives are counted in today's tradition.

It is interesting to reflect on this way of counting relatives. In the new testament frequently we read about the brothers and sisters of Jesus. It is a blood relationship that is being mentioned. The ancient Hebrews had a similar method of counting relatives. The cousins of Jesus are referred to as brothers and sisters.

A relative could always be adopted. If two girls were good friends they might adopt each other as sisters, and two men might adopt each other as brothers. Or the affection might be shared by members of different generations in which case the adoption might be in the case of women that of niece and aunt or in the case of two men that of uncle and a nephew. However, it is important to note that these adoption ceremonies involved not only the two who became related by the ceremony, but all their families. The family of the one became the family of the other and vice versa. This relationship by adoption was noted by all the members of each family. Even today on the occasion of a death, one will hear mention that the deceased was "a relative of mine by adoption" meaning that the two were members of families where an adoption had taken place. A person would have the same obligations to the adopted person as to one related by blood. It would be necessary to rejoice when some good fortune came to that adopted person as well as to grieve when illness or death struck.

In the practical order this extended family and adoption system made it always possible for some one to be responsible for the children in the case of death. There was no need for orphan asylums or social agencies to place a young child for care. No child became an orphan because of death. There was always somebody to care for the child.

When death came to the community and took a loved one or a warrior was brought back dead from battle, the burial procedure was quick. The Lakota did not bury their dead in the ground but wrapped them in hides and placed them upon a burial scaffold where raise aloft in the air in warm weather the un-embalmed body quickly disintegrated. A warriors horse sometimes would be slain at the foot of the scaffold. Tears, mourning and the keening of women were part of the ceremony. Sometimes a wife or mother would cut her hair, slash her arms or cut off the tip of her finger. She was a disheveled figure wrapped in grief mourning her dead. Later the bones would be gathered in a leather pouch and buried in the earth.

In regard to Crazy Horse, the great Lakota military strategist, his death and the record of the movement of his parents with his remains eastward to the Rosebud Sioux Indian Reservation are a matter of military record. However, on the way to Rosebud the military company stopped around the confluence of the White River, which flows eastward, and Manderson and Porcupine Creeks, which flow northward in southern South Dakota. His parents carried his remains and went south to bury them. Twenty-four hours later they returned and continued the journey to Rosebud. They never announced where his remains were buried. Descendants of Crazy Horse have indicated a knowledge of where he is buried, but those white men who have joined in digging for his remains have spent many a sweltering day under the South Dakota sun digging in vain. His remains have never been found.

There were ceremonies to assuage the grief. The Wiping of Tears brought the community together in support of the bereaved. They would offer them water to drink, something to smoke and wipe away the tears that had formed. The rite was administered directly to the individuals who suffered the loss. It was consoling.

Since the Lakotas lived in communities across the plain, each self-sufficient in securing game and gathering wild food such as choke cherries and wild turnips, there were no villages close to any other village. The community had friends among some of the other tribes, but others were hostile enemies. The sound of shouting children could be a threat to the whole community so the children were especially quiet though active in their play. A mother as a matter of habit would hold shut a child's nose when the little one cried. The child had to learn that it was essential to be as quiet as possible at all times. The result was an atmosphere of quiet that clothed their play. They did not make noise.

Even forty years ago it was possible to tell when one visited an Indian school by the quietness of children at play. Each of these rites and patterns of action were a human, cultural way of meeting with the necessities and the grief in life. The mistake was made in suspecting that the ideal of European culture was the cultural ideal toward which all should strive. That was wrong. In meeting the necessities and grief of life, one had to consider the circumstances in which people lived. The emotions of the Indians were as sincere as were the emotions of the European settlers. The Europeans and their descendants felt an obligation to have their cultural ideals arise in the Indians. Deep down within themselves both groups had similar intangibles, but on the surface they manifested themselves in different tangibles. It was joy and grief, honor and disgrace, family life and loss, the whole gamut of feeling to which we humans are heir.

CHANGES IN CULTURE

— CHAPTER VIII —

At the end of the Twentieth Century the world is experiencing changes in culture at a rate never felt before on this earth. The technology of our time is multiplying at an ever increasing rate and leaves its imprint by changing the cultures of the world. An abundance of techniques is suddenly available to all people almost everywhere. As was noted above, the abundance of snow provided the Eskimos with material to build shelters from the cold. Today the computer has become so widespread in the developed countries that children begin using them in early stages of their education and assume, until they are more correctly informed, that children have always used them. Like the snow which the Eskimos used in constructing their shelters, the computers become a natural resource for the young.

At the same time that computers are coming into greater use, other portions of the population around the earth are forced into refugee camps or communities that somehow provide for the needs of those who have had to flee their homeland. Rather than the experience of an abundance of computers, they experience a shortage of materials that their grandparents could not imagine. Their grandparents were willing to work hard and bring about a meeting of their needs. We have forming about us those who have a remarkable satisfying of their needs and those who have less for the fulfillment of their expectations. For some there is more than is needed; for others, less than is required.

While the computer brings ease and efficiency into the lives of many, the lack of basic needs runs through the lives of so many others that they do not find ease or experienced efficiency. No linking of cultural groups on the face of the earth is possible. Culture is a way of living learned informally by children from the behavior of elders in their society.

When cultures are disrupted by revolution and war, when people are forced to flee slaughter in their homelands, when natural disasters such as floods and earthquakes destroy the homes and resources of societies, changes are made in the schemes of living that had characterized the populations of the earth.

Often children become orphans who wander without parent or home before the onslaught of disaster. Elders in their community are killed, and they find themselves looking to strangers for any assistance they can give. All too often these are destitute people who have nothing to give. In bewilderment they are looking for help from others who are just a little better off than they are.

However, most children in the United States are far removed from the small communities where the elders in that society informally guided the young to an understanding of the culture into which they had been born. There are mega-cities that reach from Boston to Washington, D.C. as well as other areas of he United States. Some parents are alone rearing children. Many children are left to care for themselves. They are latchkey children. They have long hours with no guidance; they shift for themselves. They do not have elders in their community to teach them the ways of their society.

They do not know the structures of their social institutions and so wander without their guidance. They have no sense of values, cultural or moral. Often they find that the television is an entertaining device that provides hours of entertainment at the switch of a dial. Marvelous heroes sweep across the screen as in reality children could never do. The commercial advertising gyrates with power and stunning shades of color shouting the wonderful effects of breakfast cereals mixed with shamrocks, the appropriateness of a specific sport shoe on their mortal feet, the mystery of fruit flavors whirled into drinks that leave a tintinnabulation in the ears of those favored to sip its wondrous tastes, those wondrously packaged products that seize the imaginations of youth across this land and drive parents who live in the real world into brutal conflict with their children desiring the wonders of modern production. On their own, children will scheme and shrewdly concoct plans to possess these precious products from the shelves of stores down the street. They are far removed from the age of their grandparent's who generations ago learned from the older members of their community the culture of their people.

The Lakota youth today is far removed from the hunter who showed him how to craft the bow and arrows used to slay a deer. The children of the settlers learning the daily routine of farm life from their parents and grandparents are a faint memory now as farms expand into corporations and technical skills are needed in addition to honest effort. In the city where both parents have to work to provide a living for the family many children do not receive the training of their ancestors.

The significance of a television set providing lessons for children on the important goals in life strikes a questionable response in the minds of many observers. While some programs have such purposes, children usually are not attracted to them. Programs are produced to make money. They are a business. They are designed to entertain children by attracting their attention with outrageous sequences and gadgetry. Of course, it is entertaining. Children will hardly notice the difference between the cartooned sequences and the commercials that interrupt them. While there is a director for each of the programs, the director is not a community elder with an idea of guiding a child to understand a facet of the community's culture. The director, be it man or woman, is concerned about producing a program that will entrap a child's attention. The director is not concerned with the teaching of culture to children. The community is not involved. The cartoon director is concerned with the production of fascinating entertainment. The way of life that the community seeks for its children is lost in the sweep of colors and the fierce clashes between evil villains and "the good guys". This is not to suggest that there is no place for cartoon programs in lives of children, but the truth of the old adage "Moderation in all things" is evident, but not to children involved.

With more families living in urban areas, latchkey children growing in numbers as around half of today's marriages end in divorce and low paying salaries are increasing in numbers so that even couples who stay together can not provide the personal care that their children should have. The problem of providing children with experiences beyond their homes grows more severe. The number of children from poor homes who never have the opportunities to see a farm or vacation on a beach increases. Even the sight of a fireplace warmly burning logs in a home are unknown to many poor children and will leave them entranced when at last they see such a wonder. Traditions of the past are dying. In their place is want and the lack of the traditional persons to pass on a culture becomes more difficult. Children are born, but they are born into a culture far different from that into which their parents were born.

Because so much of culture is intangible, beyond the reach of senses, it is often not recognized. It can not be seen, felt, heard, tasted, smelled. It is difficult to comprehend. The structures of institutions have to be taught because they can not be sensed. The wondrous capacity of a child reaches far beyond what we normally expect. Values are intangible; they are beyond what can be sensed. Frequently there are fewer moral or religious values in their lives than in the lives of their parents. Some do not know anything of religion or moral values. They have no sense of what is acceptable behavior. When schools are afraid to teach the need for values in the lives of their pupils, incredible damage is done. The frightening statistics of children killing children are all part of this cultural breakdown.

Interesting enough George Gallup in the early 1990s took a poll on the depth of religious life in America. He found that only 13% of the population was deeply religious, but they are the happiest, most charitable, most tolerant, most ethical and most likely to seek a better society. Certainly, a definition of the term "religious" is not easily reached. It can not mean a grasp of one's own religion alone. It means a blending of religious qualities into an acceptable whole. The mixture of tolerance and love is especially indicative of a quality character, a readiness to accept others with different views and a willingness to give to those in need. If we reflect on Jesus Christ's command to "love God above all and our neighbor as ourselves", we find a close approach to this ideal.

Halloween has become the greatest event in the school year for elementary school children. "Trick or treat" has become the standard shout of children rushing from house to house seeking marvelous treats while wearing frightening costumes or the likenesses of a person involved in a murder which has caught the nation's attention. There is a rivalry to see who can out do one's peers with the most outrageous appearance. How curious? All this from a traditional celebration on the eve of All Hallows (Saints). All Saints day celebrated on November first is forgotten in the high emphasis on Halloween. It is not surprising to hear from conservative Christians that Halloween is a celebration of evil. How the change in emphasis of a single celebration has changed the whole nature of an event!

Another example of the erosion of structural institution goes back to the depression days of the 1930s when Franklin D. Roosevelt's agricultural recovery program was in operation. Part of the program paid farmers for not planting various crops. Among the recipients were some who looked upon any assistance from the government as an invasion of their independence as private farmers. They refused to cash the payment checks they received from the federal government. Good agricultural practice, whether sponsored by the government or any other organization, would be practiced but not at the price of their independence. Today when government checks go out under so many titles, it is hard to imagine citizens refusing payment on the principle of their independence. It definitely says something about our attitude toward federal assistance.

On a highly domestic level the quality of quiet which surrounded the life of Lakota people has undergone a radical change in modern times, The practice of an Indian mother, cutting off the flow of breath for her child when he cried by pressing his nostrils close so that the child would learn the need not to cry out and so possibly alert an enemy to their location, has changed. Enemy scouts or a small war party could always be in the neighborhood. Piercing cries could not be allowed. From birth, before he could reason, the Indian child learned that he must move in an atmosphere of quiet. The need for quiet is gone now. Tribes no longer have war parties moving about the prairie. A child can cry, and no threat of attack will be suffered. In response to this change no cutting off of breath at the child's cry is imposed. Quiet is no longer a quality of Indian life. This remarkable, distinctive characteristic of Indian schools has disappeared. Indian schools at recess can be as noisy as any other school today.

Perhaps, some other elements of change can be noted in the behavior of Indian children in transition to the noisy quality of deportment. Indian parents normally brought their children with them to public gatherings and meetings. They would be present at such meetings in which Elizabeth Fast Horse asked what was the worst thing that white men had brought to Indians. They would play without sound, active but not disruptive of the meeting. I was amazed at that time to note how children who would run screaming across an urban school's playground would be very quiet at Indian meetings in their community. They were learning that quiet was not a value at non-Indian events, but still had importance at Indian gatherings. Today even at Indian schools that quality of quiet is no longer present. A structural institution has changed and a cultural quality has been changed because of it.

Today Indian mothers are often employed, especially when they live in cities. Their children will often be without any parental supervision after school. Children will often turn to the television set for entertainment. The animated cartoons will usually catch their attention with the antics of Road Runner dropping an anvil off a cliff onto an unsuspecting enemy below or an indomitable champion of human rights defeating a snarling opponent and his evil followers. The fact is that English speaking television programs have such a hold on Indian children that they no longer have a desire to remain fluent in their Indian language. The language of value to Indian children is the language they hear on television. As the children mature, some will come to realize that an ability to speak their native language is important to their identity and will take classes in Lakota or other native Indian language, but by that time it is difficult to become fluent in a new language. Altering the institutional structures, in this case the use of a non-native language, has again altered the tangible qualities of their culture.

The most significant change in the adjustment of institutional structures in recent years has undoubtedly been the introduction of gaming casinos on Indian land. As it advances, it appears to be making incredible changes in the lives of Indian people whose tribe has established gaming casinos.

Where the lack of income was a major deficiency in the lives of many Indians, the Osage of Oklahoma were an exception because of the oil discovered under their land, many now have a more than adequate income because of the casinos. The importance of being able to manage that money is a significant consideration. The importance of managing money might well have been taught to all American Indians. It was not, on the assumption that everyone knew how to handle money. Not every one did.

When one considers whatever influence the right hemisphere of the brain or other psychological influence that produces such an effect on the Indians so that they have a creative, intuitive, visionary view of life, the need for this sort of economic training is seen. However, as the Osage were able to survive the influx of money that oil brought them, the Indians who are rich from casino operations will also be able to survive. Originally some of the oil rich Indians bought excessively luxurious possessions merely for the joy of owning them, but they settled into a more routine adjustment to their income as time passed. Decades have passed since the Osage bought to show off wealth. Modern Indians have adjusted to the influences of modern society. To date there have been no reports of spending by Indians who have casino income that is comparable to that of the Osage.

Many Indian tribes have the benefit of increased income because of the gambling casinos on their trust land, However, not all tribes have income from gaming on Indian land. For those who do have gaming income, new responsibilities in regard to that money arise.

A most practical matter in this question of casino income has to do with politics and the election of government officials. Now contributions to election campaigns are sought from those Indians tribes who have such income. It is significant. People who actively support a candidate or a party with funds have a louder voice in that campaign. Consequently they have a louder voice in the functioning of government. To move from a place outside the government where one is not even a citizen, but a member of a "domestic, dependent nation" as Chief Justice John Marshall described their situation in 1831 in his decision in the settling the case of the Cherokee Nation v. Georgia is most significant.

The fact that Indians were not citizens of the United States of America might also be considered. Legally even the Fourteenth Amendment was declared not applicable to American Indians in the case of Elk v. Wilkins, a suit decided in 1884 in Omaha, Nebraska in which John Elk, an Indian who had separated himself from his tribe sought in the courts his right to vote in the elections of the United States. The court found that he was a human being within the meaning of that word as used by the courts but that he was declared not to be a citizen of the United States. This happened eight years after the celebration of the first centennial of the Declaration of Independence, which, as has been noted, was seriously marred by the victory of the Sioux and Cheyenne at the Battle of the Little Big Horn in Montana.

Some note should be given to the long slow process by which American Indians became citizens of the United States of America. Relations were established between the Indian tribes on the east coast of this country and the colonizing European powers establishing their first foot holds. Treaties, the normal form of solemn relationship between nations, were then ratified and signed by representatives of the European power and the various Indian tribes or nations. Once the United States of America was established, it took responsibility for the European signatories in regard to the Indian tribes. The United States in its turn signed treaties which the Constitution of the United States in Article Six called "the supreme law of the land".

Only on March 3, 1871 in an obscure rider to an appropriations bill did the policy of treaties come to an end. Humanitarian groups protested the policy and the House of Representatives found that the Senate, because of their right to approve treaties with other nations and tribes, had too much control of Indian affairs. The enactment of this legislation ended the signing of treaties.

Indians were not granted citizenship when the United States was founded. They lived within this land as independent nations who were members of their tribes. The Allotment Act of 1887, also known as the Dawes Act, granted citizenship to Indians who followed the prescriptions of the act and in effect left their tribes. Finally in 1924, seventy years ago, United States citizenship was granted to all Indians. This was largely in recognition of the generous service of American Indians during the First World War. The tradition of the honorable warrior remained alive in the tribes and found in this warfare, much more severe than in their old form of warfare where counting coup was so important, an opportunity to realize some of the old tradition.

However, with passage of the 1924 law Indians did not automatically receive the full rights of a citizen of the United States. Many states passed various laws that made voting impossible for the new citizens. Various laws regarding poll taxes, property taxes and other matters made it impossible for Indians to go to a balloting place and vote for their favorite candidate for public office. Only in 1958 were the last of these state laws struck down in court, and the Indian finally had the right to vote. That was only 18 years before the United States celebrated its 200 anniversary of the signing of the Declaration of Independence. Clearly the United States declared "that all men are created equal", but

71

Indians, black slaves and Orientals somehow did not fit easily into that statement. It was originally a land for white Europeans. Benjamin Franklin, George Washington and Thomas Jefferson had a deep interest in the Six Nations of the Iroquois Confederacy and used principles from it in establishing the United States government, but politics never allowed them to name Indians citizens of the United States. Only 182 years later did all obstacles to that right fall, and Indians were finally real citizens of the United States. The principles of our citizenship had finally prevailed over our actual practice.

Interestingly enough, American Indians are the only population in the United States who legally possess dual citizenship. Congress granted them citizenship and did not demand that they renounce their tribal citizenship. Aliens from foreign countries after proper preparation are admitted to United States citizenship with the renouncing of their citizenship in whatever land they held it. Indians are citizens or members of their tribes which are far older than the United States, and they are citizens of the United States. Curiously, this puts them in the position of dealing with their own nation on treaty rights which are normally handled by Congress. They are in the United States a most unique people. All the arguments by those who are jealous of the fishing and hunting and wild food gathering rights have to understand the complicated history that finally resulted in their citizenship in the United States despite the efforts by some states to obstruct their full rights to citizenship.

A further note on the legality of Indian gaming is in order. The laws and judicial decisions of this country allow Indian tribes, who are recognized as nations in the sense that the United States of America used that term and whose treaties are with the federal government, to practice any form of gaming that is allowed by the individual state anywhere in its jurisdiction. The state is not allowed to discredit the tribe. It does not have that jurisdiction. However, recent federal laws require that the state and tribe enter into a contract of agreement for the establishment of the more elaborate forms of gaming. Sometimes years are spent in discussion of terms or the imposition of terms by the state. A few states are truly reluctant to enter into contracts of agreement.

In California the Cabazon Indian Band began a card room operation like many others throughout the state. The difference here was that no money went to the state. It went to the Cabazon government. California brought suit to gain its right to a tax on the profits. It ended with a decision by the United States Supreme Court in 1987 that stated the Cabazons had the right to self-government and control of gaming operations on their reservation.

States seem inclined to favor supporting non-Indian gaming but are reluctant to give the same support to Indian tribes. Tribes have legally established many gaming casinos across the country on Indian trust land, that is land held in trust for the tribe by the federal government through the Department of the Interior. They are making a profit. Some non-Indian gamblers resent Indians and their gaming operations and have brought suit in federal court arguing that the federal law has been too lenient with them. Thus far the Indian tribes have been successful in winning these cases.

Indian people have a natural instinct for gambling. In more traditional days they did not have the wealth to accumulate large monetary winnings. When tribes, like the Lakotas, had no medium of exchange, they had to gamble with property that they owned - horses, buffalo robes, items of that nature. In more recent times it has become necessary for schools, located close together on an Indian reservation, no longer to play basketball games because of the irresponsible wagering among local people on the outcome of the games. However, the biggest betters in Indian casinos are the people from off the reservations who come to gamble.

Obviously the various tribes have different returns on their gaming investment. Some tribes are small and members receive a larger return that those who have many members. Moreover, the board of directors is able to allot funding to schools, charitable organizations and other similar agencies. One of the biggest names in gambling has brought suit against a Connecticut tribe which is the biggest threat to his own casinos, on the charge that the government has given Indians more than their due share in gaming operations. At least with the tribes, members divide the profits, whereas all the profits go to him when the Indians are excluded.

The days of buffalo hunts are over. Some Indians are fitting into the world of modern America. Others are making the effort to change. Still others are lost, often in a world of alcohol and drugs.

When we look to Alaska, that massive state which is more than twice the size of Texas, we see the native populations there, Eskimos, Indians and Aleuts, each group insisting on its distinction from the others so that the only common term to embrace them is the Alaska native people. Government, as in all cases involving minority groups, has interfered with their development. The institutional structures of their society have been altered.

Some have left Alaska and have established themselves away from home in the other forty-nine states. The majority remain in Alaska. There are 86,000 individuals, all United States citizens, who live in the richest state in the union but are facing social impairments at incomprehensible rates.

Changes have come too rapidly. Traditions have not been able to adapt to the changes and have lost their ability to guide the people of the Eskimo, Indian and Aleut cultures. Whether willingly or unwillingly, the direction of life has been given over to outside forces. They are like the latchkey child who turns to the overwhelming force of television for cultural formation.

MUSEUM PIECES
— CHAPTER IX —

Today the technical advancements made in our culture are considered signs of progress. Sometimes in reflecting on the changes made in the Lakota culture observers are concerned about Indians moving beyond their cultural limits when they did not know what settlers would bring. There is regret about how difficult rapid change has been for them. Such changes have been a challenge, but it is good to recognize that they are human beings who can progress in cultural changes as well as any other group. They will wonder when first they experience advanced technology and may require a generation or two to accept such advancements, but there are many advancements that they can accept without difficulty. The gun is an example. Though they wore clothes of leather, they were able marksmen with the gun. It did not take generations to accept this technical advance.

The horse is another example of remarkable adaptation in a very short time. The modern horse is not native to the American hemispheres. Spaniards brought them to this country in the sixteenth century. In one way or another Indian tribes obtained horses for their own use. They were abandoned; they were stolen; there was natural increase. Some tribes made use of them. The Lakotas became lords of the plains by mastering the horse. More than many tribes, they made the horse a part of their culture. In fact it is hard for us today to think of their life without the horse.

Life was changed because of horses. They were cherished. Lakota men grew up with the horse and adjusted their skills to the qualities the horse exhibited. They did not have guns, but they had horses that swept across the prairie and enhanced their form of warfare.

The herds increased. They began to change their way of life. Horses were given to the father of a young woman sought for marriage. The favorite horse of a warrior was killed as a sign of grief at his death. It lay below his burial scaffold eloquently speaking of the passage from life to death. When the tribe moved, the entire tribe moved with a speed that had been unknown to their ancestors. Where travois would be placed on the backs of large dogs and slowly dragged to a new camp site, they now had horses to pull the travois carrying a full tipi and a load of household goods. Children would ride on them. Women's work was eased.

As the forefathers of America struggled with the burden of colonialism under a European power and were preparing to sign the Declaration of Independence, the Lakotas burst upon the rolling northern plains, a force dominating all movement. They were the masters of the plains.

They had one century to give new meaning to their culture. They so adapted their way of living to the sleek, swift horses that many do not realize they had ever lived without them. From 1776 to 1887 when the skilled military leader Crazy Horse was killed at Fort Robinson in what is now Nebraska and the tribes were placed on reservations, they ruled the plains.

They had but one century. And in that one hundred years they entranced the imagination of Europe and the world. The colorful Indian garb of leather and fur, woven porcupine quills accenting as with paint the lines of dress, bold eagle feathers and soft plums from meadowlarks and other prairie birds swirled around lean bodies dancing or painted for war when, as sailing sloops, they charged across a sea of grass.

They were men of honor as they encountered the settlers who had no grasp of the meaning their way of life held for them. The settlers had no time for men who had no time but to ride the plains. Life was hard. They struggled to establish a life such as they had seen in Europe but with the freedom they saw in their dream of America. The settlers were more powerful.

The reservation rose. The Indian scheme of life died. Definite boundaries were set beyond which no Indian could go. They were like prisoners in their native land. The government was late in sending rations; it was a ploy to force Indians into compliance with their orders.

In the winter of 1875-76 thousands of Indians left the reservations to hunt food. The buffalo herds were already reduced in size, but the huge animals could be found. Many Lakotas and Cheyennes were gathered in Montana when General Custer came out from Fort Abraham Lincoln in North Dakota to drive them by force to the reservations. At the Little Big Horn River he met the Indians and was overwhelmed by a legion of Indians. His military unit was wiped out to the last man.

Slowly they returned to the reservations, defeated. For the men there was no future. Traditionally they set the example. They were the warrior-hunters. Now there was no warfare. There was no hunting. Cattle were driven in from Texas and in a mock attempt to recreate the old days were turned lose at the distribution grounds for Indians to kill as they had killed buffalo, riding along side, shooting a bow, throwing a lance.

Interestingly enough some of the Mexican cattle drovers who herded the cattle to the Indians were attracted to their way of life, married Lakota women and allowed their blood to mingle with the next Lakota generation. They never returned to Mexico.

For a century Indians had known a way of life that met their needs and encouraged their feelings. Then came the reservations. Defeat galled them. They were helpless to rise against it. Indian warriors saw no purpose in living. They got drunk on what little whiskey they could get. Later their would be an abundance of alcohol and they would become alcoholic. Tuberculosis became a disease in their midst. They became subjects for some psychiatrists studying the effects of sudden changes in life styles.

Women became the usual spokespersons for the family when they met with a white official. Even until the second Wounded Knee, they were most likely to carry on the conversation when an Indian couple met with some person of prominence in their community. Boys began life in innocence, but by the time they were of middle school age, a sense of futility overwhelmed them. They were about to become Indian men and their was no longer any place in Indian life for Indian men.

In 1890 Indians were first counted in the United States Census. They totaled less than 250,000 persons. Undoubtedly that was not an accurate figure, but it gave a good idea of the Indian loss. There had been millions when Europeans first came to this land. Now they were called the "vanishing Americans". Soon they would all be gone. It has not worked out that way. Today there are over two million Indians in this country. They are Americas fastest growing population.

Perhaps it takes a century for each change to run its course. With the coming of the horse the Lakotas life swept upward in glorious light. A century later it crashed, disconnected in every way. A century later in 1973 when the second occupation of Wounded Knee occurred, a notable change also took place. Alcoholism is still a problem, but there are organizations working against that. Many Indians are going on to college, although some still do drop out of high school. R. C. Gorman and other Indian artists are an important segment of the American art scene. The American Indian Dance Theater is traveling about the country producing a spectacular scene of traditional dances.

On the political scene there has been change. Every president has shifted programs as he came into office and ended by not accomplishing what he sought. However, today Indians have found their way to the courts and have won significant legal battles. Some Indians have won their way into Congress and have usually been besieged by all the tribes in America to advance their treaty rights.

A people who have had to face so many political changes, to make so many adjustments, to meet so many challenges of the dominant society, deserve a lot of respect for not ending up in total chaos. They have a quality that stems from their tradition. They have done remarkably well for a people who have had the horse lead them on a heady ride only to have limits placed on their movements. There are many museum pieces in their history. There are many advances being made in their lives.

Unless we are able to recognize human ability to advance with technology, we run the risk of dating cultures and judge them by their progress in advancing to technological superiority. Cultural groups do not need advance technology to live a rich life. Without electricity and running water the Lakotas lived a meaningful life rich in art and military skills, with dedicated relationships that warmly bound the members of a community, and with appreciation of literature, although they had no written language.

I never grasped the idea of epic poetry being the start of all poetry until I lived with the Indians. The Crow man who was my neighbor told me once of the epic poetry that his people had. It was not written but passed along in oral form. It struck me as being equal to the Greeks in its scope of activity and wandering. Even the *deus ex machina* devices used to resolve a dilemma were employed.

One poem recounted a warrior going off to battle and the complications that result from wounds received in battle. Here it is necessary to remember that the Crow people were related to the Lakotas by a similarity in language although they considered them to be enemies. The group of warriors who sought glory in their encounters with an enemy had the same notion of warfare that the Lakotas had. There was no organized militia sent by the tribe, but a group of six or so warriors seeking to prove their valor. The poem describes their going on the warpath. Then at a far distance from home, as the hero seeks to count coup, he is wounded by the enemy. His leg is broken. He is seriously injured and unable to move home. His brother, who is one of the warriors, hides him and cares as best he can to his needs. Above all these injuries, he is in love and is unable to return home to his beloved. Finally, as he is recovering, he persuades his brother to make the long journey home and return with the girl he loves. He makes a shelter for his wounded brother so he has protection during the weeks of his absence. He surrounds him with food and then leaves him to recover as he departs for home.

This epic poem goes on to describe the demanding undertakings that the young woman and her lover's brother endure in their search for him. At one time they encounter an enemy tribe camping in their path. So as to avoid detection, they fasten branches in their hair and slowly crawl up a hill that will give them a view of the enemy camp below. At last they find the wounded warrior. The two lovers are reunited. He has improved in health because of the provisions that his brother has made for him. He is ready to return home with them.

This epic poem with its elevated style and oral tradition narrates the story taken from the adventures of a people and thrilled countless listeners as it was passed on from generation to generation. The facility to memorize this and other poems was unquestionably aided by the fact that there was no written account of this epic. The need for accuracy in telling the poem, unlike a lay written version, would be evident to all who listened. They knew what was to be expected in its telling whereas a written version may have allowed errors. The reader would not know what to expect.

Today this has been lost. Alcoholism has taken its toll of such ability. Television has offered a more passive view of what has taken the place of art. The talent of a people is overlooked without any grief at its passing.

However, for many of other cultures the view of the Indian is usually wrapped in these accounts of the past and there is a reluctance to allow Indians to progress. They make Indians a museum piece, snatched from history and displayed for the viewers of the modern scene. Obviously, the clothing and shelter, the foods and weapons, all that is necessary for a scheme of life should be preserved in museums and recounted in books, but it is important to allow the modern descendants of this culture to be free to move on in life as they find it. One should never be caught in the web of time so that modern viewers expect Indians always to wear "feathers in their hair".

Indians, as everyone else, will look to the past for identification. It is important to know who we are and from whom we come, what our ancestors did and taught. The quality of being an ancestor or an elder, either in family or in the community, gave that member an aura of authority that was respected by those who held a lesser stature. Culture has always come from those who have gone before the present generation.

As Indians were members of tribes, the distinctiveness of the tribes will be a part of their heritage. The existence of some five hundred tribes in this country when the Europeans first came reminds us that their is a plurality in their identity. Each tribe was distinct, sometimes widely distinct. Others had similar traditions. For example the Lakotas divided into seven sub-tribes, the Oglalas, the Brules, the Minniconjous, the Hunkpapas, the Two Kettles, the No Bows (or San Arcs) and the Blackfeet who are not to be confused with the Blackfeet tribe of Montana.

Originally the seven tribes were probably one Lakota tribe, but through the years divided into these seven tribes. One factor that is responsible for this division is the fact that the Lakota used a system of total consensus in their councils of government. Normally, there were no time constraints. A discussion could take days if it were necessary. Agreement of those involved had to be reached, or there was no agreement. The point being discussed would simply be put aside because there was no agreement. Total agreement was essential. Consequently, tribes were conservative in making any changes in their operation.

However, on some occasions there was a point of difference that led to a separation of tribal members. Agreement could not be reached. Those in support of a change felt so strongly about the issue that they left the parent tribe. Seldom was there any animosity between the tribes. They merely had different points of view on some issue and divided. Socially some division like this was necessary. In their simple life style they did not have the technology to provide for an ever increasing number of people. A tribe had to have a sufficient number of members to be effective in providing for the welfare of all its members, but there could be too many. It was loyalty to the tribe that was essential for tribal operations in a largely forbidden area where enemy tribes might always be encountered or natural disasters might occur.

At this point a look at tribal sense of history is appropriate. Since they had no written history, the oral accounts of significant events was important as well as the tradition of Winter Counts. A Winter Count consisted of figures painted consecutively every winter on a buffalo robe indicating the most significant event that had occured during the past year. It might be a spectacular showing of a comet or shower of meteors in the sky, a multiple birth to a woman of the tribe, the arrival of an important visitor or group of visitors, the death of a significant leader of the tribe or any other event that seemed important at the time of painting. A Winter Count listed the recent events that the tribe experienced.

Oral history was not chronological but episodic. Events that the tribe experienced would be recounted in a manner similar to the telling of stories or poems. A greater emphasis on details would be noted. For example tales of battle at the Little Big Horn River would note that a warrior rode a roan colored horse in his attack on the enemy that day. The shape of a mountain would be distinctive and so described or the extent of a prairie fire sweeping across the plains would be recounted. Wild animals scurrying from its deadly wake of scorched earth would be recounted. They knew who they were and what had happened to their ancestors to make them distinctive from all the other tribes about them. Some parts of their history was shared with other tribes, for example, the events in the skies or prairie fires, but other episodes were strikingly their own. The wise man would reflect on the significance of these episodes and be ready when some similar event was about to occur. To know history, even when it does not follow the chronological form we know today, is to be prepared.

When the occupation of Wounded Knee took place under the leadership of the American Indian Movement in 1973, recognition of Lakota history was obvious. There were other towns such as Manderson, Kyle and Allen that might have been occupied, but none of them had the history of Wounded Knee where around three hundred Lakota men, women and children had been slaughtered. At the site, where in 1890 such a defeat was endured, the new stand for Indian rights would be made.

The imagination of the world was electrified as Indians gathered in conflict surrounding the scattered hamlet of Wounded Knee. Again, the United States sent in military men who used military weaponry in their approach. The flag of the United States was flown upside down as a sign of distress. Shots were fired and men were killed and injured as the struggle went on. The town was surrounded, and in the evening from U.S. Highway 18 the sight of magnesium flares floating downward in the northern skies suggested the worst of modern warfare. There was no peace on the Pine Ridge Reservation.

What had caused this battle?

Many factors were involved, but I can relate from my own experience one incident of domestic Indian significance that influenced Wounded Knee.

At Oglala, South Dakota, was a government Indian school with a progressive population concerned about the education of their children. They recognized themselves as Indian and wanted an Indian twist to the education their children received. They incorporated an organization called Oyate, that is "the people" or "the nations" in Lakota. Its purpose was to present the Lakota history and tradition to the children at the Oglala Indian School and also at Red Cloud Indian School which is operated by the Jesuits and Franciscan Sisters, volunteers and Indian staff at Holy Rosary Mission. Both schools enrolled children from the Oglala community. The U. S. Department of Health, Education and Welfare, as that department was known in the early 1970s, provided an annual grant of $125,000.00 to Oyate. They used the money totally for educational purposes. None of the member of the Board of Directors receive any remuneration, except the joy of seeing their youth take pride in being Indian. That emotion ran so deep that no amount of money could possibly pay for the privilege of serving on the board.

I, a non-Indian, was vice-president and the only non-Indian on the board, because federal law required that such organizations be open to members of various racial backgrounds. I still consider it an honor to have been invited by the Oyate committee to be the sole non-Indian member of the board and then to have been elected vice-president.

Slowly we began to make progress. We began to prepare Indian education programs to be used first at the Oglala school and the next year at Red Cloud Indian School. We hired Calvin Jumping Bull, a college graduate and experienced educator as director of the program. We discussed our wishes and agreed to allow him to hire staff to carry out this Indian program. The staff set up a program of interviewing elders in the community on the traditions of the Lakota people. These interviews were preserved on audio tape so that they might be reused and provide a definite statement from specific, respected individuals.

From the materials on these tapes programs were begun for

the kindergarten classes. New tapes were made especially for the children at the kindergarten level. Sheets were made and duplicated for the use of the children on Indian subjects contained in the tapes. The Indian kindergarten classes colored pictures of feathers and animals of the area, traditional ceremonies, tipis and Indian dress, traditional children playing games, anything that the Lakota tradition had to offer.

The program was a success. It influenced the children to take pride in being Indian. The attractive scenes and artifacts used by traditional Lakota people, the animals, their homes, warriors on swift horses, women busy with the work of the home were all indications to them of the importance of being Lakota. Children enjoyed coloring the Indian subjects. Children began to take pride in being Indian.

A staff member was provided to both schools by Oyate to present the program to the kindergarten children at the Oglala School and to the Montessori children at Red Cloud Indian School. Each year another program would be prepared for the next grade with the appropriate advancement for that grade.

Oyate was a success because it provided the means for Indian children on the reservation to progress in school while happily accepting themselves as Indian. Children were happy to be Indian. Then an election took place on the Pine Ridge Indian Reservation that made a tragic change in this program.

Richard Wilson was elected President of the Oglala Sioux Tribe. He objected to the people of Oglala receiving $125,000.00 annually from the federal government. His thought was that the money should go to the Oglala Sioux Tribe. He wrote to the Department of Health, Education and Welfare and asked to have the money sent to the tribal government. There was some hesitation on the part of the department since they thought that the program was successful. They agreed that no one on their staff was well acquainted with Indians. Probably they should not make the decision. They sought the opinion of the Department of the Interior in whose structure was the Bureau of Indian Affairs. Some time was spent before a decision was made.

Wilson argued that the central government of the tribe was being undermined as long as individual groups, such as Oyate, could obtain funding from the federal government. All such funds should go to the tribal government. All Oyate could argue was that the program was a success and should possibly be spread to other schools on the reservation. They felt that it would be better for the parents of the children and the community in which they lived to receive funding for the program.

In late 1972 the Department of the Interior recommended that the Department of Health, Education and Welfare provide the funding for Oyate to the Oglala Sioux Tribe. The members of Oyate felt betrayed. They would not be able to continue in an organized way their program to train Indian children to be happy being Indian.

Oyate had one final meeting as 1972 drew to an end. Of all the meetings I have attended over the years and which often remain a blur in my memory, I shall never forget that final meeting of Oyate. I especially remember the president, Max Blacksmith, reflect on the impact the program had on his family. He mentioned that his daughter had not had the benefit of the program. She was always a little uncomfortable in accepting herself as Indian. His son on the other hand was younger and had participated in the program at the Oglala school. He was happy to be Indian. He never had any contrary feelings to contradict his identity. He was only in the early years of elementary school, but he knew who he was and he was ready to face the world as a Lakota. What more could we ask of an educational program?

We talked about the future. The American Indian Movement was already active in western South Dakota and the suggestion was made that we might call AIM for support in our disagreement with Wilson. That was the end of the meeting. That was the end of Oyate.

The President of the Oglala Sioux Tribe did not take over the program that Oyate had begun. He put the money into the tribal treasury. It was used for whatever expenses were at hand. Those whom Oyate had hired were out of work. They had no value in the eyes of the tribal president.

Among the people who were unemployed was Calvin Jumping Bull. I hired him to be the Assistant Principal at Red Cloud Indian School. It was a mid-year appointment. At the end of that year he became Principal of the school where his ideas had an enduring effect. He started the annual celebration of Chief Red Cloud Day at the school on December 10th, the anniversary of his death in 1909. He recognized in Red Cloud a determined Lakota who would not surrender to the United States. Red Cloud had avoided meetings of the government's Peace Commission until in the summer of 1868 the United States agreed to his terms. It removed forces from the government forts from the Powder River country where they would protect the Union Pacific railroad as it moved westward through Montana. It dismantled and burned the military structures. Finally in November, 1868 he signed the treaty. He had won this battle and reaped the victory.

No one was hired by Wilson to carry on the Indian program in the schools.

Late in February, 1973 in the evening of the day that Ben Black Elk, who for years posed at Mount Rushmore in his Indian garb was buried, the American Indian Movement came into Wounded Knee and occupied the community. For a night it held hostages among whom were the Gildersleeves who ran the Trading Post at Wounded Knee. They did not know that Mrs. Gildersleeve and her brother were registered members of the Chippewa Tribe in Minnesota. When the leaders realized that she and her brother who operated the museum at Wounded Knee were relatives of the AIM leader Dennis Banks who was also

Black Elk 1937

Photo by W. Ben Hunt ©Mrs. Jean Krainik

from Minnesota, they were puzzled. The next morning with the federal government announcing that the leadership faced federal kidnapping charges, they released their hostages.

AIM had informed the press of the planned occupation and so had coverage of their activities from the very start. The military and the news media came rushing to Wounded Knee. It proved how ill prepared the news media was in covering an Indian event. For the first weeks reporters followed the "Indian warriors" as they moved about the community. They could respond to the press conferences that the AIM leaders called. Every point that an Indian leader wanted to have mentioned on the nightly television news was sure to be reported.

That the occupation of Wounded Knee was a debatable subject seems not to have reached the minds of most reporters there. When the residents of Wounded Knee who were opposed to the occupation of their community gathered their cars and pickups together, loaded them with their belongings' and drove around the community several times to let those who were looking for news that they were unhappy with the occupation, the news media did not grasp what was happening. These residents of Wounded Knee left the occupied Wounded Knee and sought shelter with their relatives and friends until the federal government brought in mobile homes for their use.

Another factor in this issue with the press was a practice that news agencies had of not allowing a reporter to remain longer than two weeks with a story. The fear was that there was danger that one side or the other might be influencing the reporter's story. However, the Indian communities were so far removed from the newsmen's understanding that in two weeks they might only begin to see what the situation really was.

However, they were replaced, and the new reporters began trying to understand the operation and they, in turn, were replaced by fresh media personnel.

At Holy Rosary Mission and other outlets on the reservation there was always bead work for sale. It was a cottage industry. Men and women would fashion medallions and daisy chains, bolo ties and beaded combs and bring them in for sale. All the bead work was sold out during the occupation. Reporters and military alike wanted something they could take home.

Meanwhile, the response of the world press was amazing. There were few phones on the reservation. Many of the calls came to the office at Holy Rosary Mission where in a few minutes they wanted an account of several hundred years of cultural conflict. The intangibles of culture: the invisible forces at work on both groups; the difficulty of understanding what had been grasped from birth by the Indians were involved in a proper answer.

Meanwhile AIM had become confused in its purpose at Wounded Knee. Many locals had believed that AIM came in response to calls to replace the policies of Dick Wilson. But with all the media coverage AIM began to talk of a history of betrayal, denial of treaty rights and the whole involved misunderstanding of the other's culture or scheme of living.

At night Indians came in and out of Wounded Knee. They avoided the barrier that the military tried to string around the area. The roads were solidly closed, but routes lay open along the creek bottoms and wooded land. They brought in food and supplies. The occupation went on.

Finally in May when the effects of venereal disease grew to intolerable proportions, the two months of defiance seemed to be going nowhere and media coverage had all but disappeared, an agreement on the part of the leadership to meet with government representatives at Pierre, the state capital. They met; they talked; they never met again. It was a face saving affair. Hours of otherwise unavailable television coverage had been given to Indian issues. The nation, in fact the world, had some insight into the challenges of Indians, but little effect was realized.

When election time came around again, Russell Means ran against Dick Wilson, the incumbent president. Prior to that time no incumbent had ever been reelected to office. Because Means in his campaign talked so strongly about returning to the old days, replacing doctors with medicine men in the hospitals, turning off the electricity that was purchased from the white world, getting rid of white money and other white products, he scared the voters. A woman once said to me, "Russell wants us to go back to washing clothes in the creek." They did not want to wash clothes in the creek. They reelected Dick Wilson.

The world at large did not have a grasp of Indian culture. But some changes can be counted; whether because of Wounded Knee or on the occasion of Wounded Knee, is not so clear. With the help of the federal government Indian colleges were established on the reservations and have had an important effect on the lives of the people. Twenty eight schools of higher learning were begun. Before Wounded Knee, there were hardly twenty-five Indians who were attorneys, now there are over six thousand across the country, many serving their own tribes. Non-profit legal firms have been established and take on cases of tribes that have been ignored for more than a century. Some cases come to the United States Supreme Court and are usually resolved in favor of the tribe.

Where there were only a few Indians who were M.D.s before Wounded Knee, today we find more than five hundred Indians who are Doctors practicing medicine on reservations and in private practice. In other fields there are many Indians with degrees from prominent universities, but in the field of art a refreshing group of Indian artists have appeared. Each summer the annual Red Cloud Indian Art Show at Pine Ridge, now with more than twenty-five years of exhibits to its credit, has been a distinguished pioneer of such shows.

The culture of the Indians has changed considerably during the years that have followed Wounded Knee. The impact of the modern world has had an explosive effect upon them. More than half of the Indian population now lives off the reservations, largely in urban areas where generally they live in close proximity to one another.

But what was the effect on the Pine Ridge Reservation? The reservation was divided right from the start on the occupation of Wounded Knee. Some of that division remains to this day. Immediately after the end of hostilities a series of murders were committed. Some who supported the occupation, including Indians from outside the reservation, were killed and left lying where they fell. Others who supported Dick Wilson and members of what was called the "Goon Squad", a para-military organization he established to protect himself and his interests, were in turn murdered. None of these murder cases has been resolved, except for Leonard Peltier who was sentenced to two life terms for killing two FBI agents at Oglala, South Dakota. The evidence used against him was at best questionable. His appeals for a new trial have always been denied.

The effects were felt at Pow Wows which are traditionally times of celebration and festivities. Immediately after Wounded Knee attendance at Pow Wows was drastically reduced. Those who did attend never spoke of Wounded Knee because no one wanted to be identified with either side. After the murders ceased there was an increase in attendance, but a continual silence on the Wounded Knee occupation remains.

However, the Pow Wows themselves have left the reservations and have become spectacular events in the large cities of the country. There are, of course, local Pow Wows held simply for the joy of dancing in traditional dress. The feathers used today are chemically dyed and have a brilliance that their ancestors would not recognize. Modern cloths are also used and the amplification system is essential for every dance. One of the major changes now lies in the fact that each dancer is identified by a number that is irreverently displayed on the dancers attire much as is worn by rodeo performers. The Pow Wows are no longer just for the fun of traditional dancing; they are a competition in which judges decide who are the best dancers. They are awarded prizes for their performances and will mention the award in their resumes if that will assist them in seeking a position where Indian identity is considered.

Again there is change, and as the activity of Indians in the modern world becomes more and more accepted, the museum pieces of their traditional lives is more and more removed from their experiences today. Dress, transportation, housing, recreation, language, occupations have been transformed. It is hard to hang on to the rigid forms of traditions when so much of daily life is altered. Sometimes there is mention that Red Cloud or Sitting Bull or some other famous leader of the past is a direct ancestor of a particular person, but the traditional form of warfare which was so necessary in the way of living and the establishment of male prominence, is so removed from military warfare today that its significance is seldom grasped.

So many people have no idea of how the life of the Indian man has changed since the settlers first moved among them. Traditionally he was a warrior-hunter. He ranged far from home and counted coup. He provided meat for the members of his family and community. He was elected to the tribal council where he listened for days to discussion on a question that had to be decided by all the members present. When faced with a task, he would work all day, not only during day lit hours, but into the night, struggling with a prairie fire, fighting enemies, hunting animals, working on preparations for winter. When that was finished he would be ready to relax, dance, enjoy his family and friends for a couple of days. He had worked. Sweat ran off his body. It was good to be home.

There was no thought of working steadily from nine to five each day with a break at the week end. The nature of his life did not allow for that routine which serves the needs of business rather than the life experience of the employee. Even today when the call for fire fighters to tackle the nations forest fires goes out, Indian men come running, youths will lie about their age as they respond to a need they understand. They will be working and not for eight hours a day. They work around the clock. They get a sandwich and coffee on the run and a chance to rest when the wind comes from a new direction. The Indian male is involved in the struggle against the devastating fire for as long as it takes.

Non-Indians may refer to him as "a lazy, drunken Indian", but in this exhausting work he is there all day, day after day, until the fire is out. They are not lazy. They are not drunk. They are responding to the work they understand. For a week or two they are traditional Indians. Are they museum pieces working in a modern world?

IDEALS AND INSTITUTIONS

— CHAPTER X —

In a society, intangibles are frequently at the root of what members of that culture seek. Culture rises from intangibles -- intangibles in an individual's life and in the life of a community. It is personal, yet shared with other members of that community. However, the cultural effect of the personal and the communal will have a different nature. For an individual the goal which is sought will first of all be comprehended in an intangible state. It will be grasped by the mind as a goal. From there the person can realize it in a concrete state. For example, an individual may want to be a skilled horseback rider. That skill is intangible as it is imagined, but it will become real with practice and repetition.

The structure of institutions exists in a society of people who have established a culture or scheme of living that provides for a unity of life and a progress in that society. There is usually some relation between the two. However, the force of the intangible upon the tangible events of life is what is important The unseen influences that which is seen. The spiritual reaches into daily life and produces the visible elements of existence.

To use the example of horseback riding again, it is only when a large number of members in that society become skilled horse-back riders that the group will be recognized for that skill. The Lakota people had no knowledge of horses until Europeans brought them to this country. Individual Lakota men envisioned themselves as masterful horseback riders and so achieve that quality. When most of the men became skilled riders that became a tangible part of their culture.

Among the people of the world there are heroes as there are cowards. Both experience the same forces of life about them, but the hero is committed to the ideal of loving care for another or others while the coward is concerned with self-preservation. A hero grows to adulthood with the notion that those around him have a value that is important. He loves them. He respects them. He may not agree with them, but if they are in danger, he will work to rescue them. The hero charges into a burning building to rescue his daughter or son. In the course of war, men and women who are truly committed to an ideal will throw themselves on a live grenade to protect others from its explosion. Mere animals will not make a sacrifice or risk the threat of death. An animal that has had the experience of affection, because of that affection, may run in to a burning building to make a rescue but in most cases will howl painfully as the structure is engulfed in flames.

Cowards have a similar relationship to a daughter or son or the other community members. Somehow the care is not so deep, the love is not so strong. The fear that all experience in seeing the flames or the live grenade reach deeper into the cowards life and he will not risk it to flame or explosion. Often enough such acts of courage or heroism are not publicly recognized, but on occasion there will be a public award for "heroism above and beyond the call of duty". Such a phrase, "above and beyond the call of duty", suggests that in the culture in which it is used there is an expectation of heroism that is within the call of duty.

Breaking into the details of heroism is difficult. Suffice to recognize that there are challenges to which a hero responds. The coward, on the other hand, has not reached so deeply into the spiritual, intangible values of a culture and does not respond. Both have faced the same threat, but have reacted differently because of their grasp of the intangibles. This is not to say that the coward does not suffer from his indecision. He suffers greatly trying to make up his mind.

The institutions of society are based on community members grasping an intangible, a spiritual quality. There is an appreciation of a value, a thing of the spirit, that will lead to an action. Individuals may rise in response and reach the role of hero. These institutional structures provide a way for society to achieve the goals it has recognized.

Twenty-five years ago I had a conversation with a Lakota woman who was the mother of several children. Her children were enrolled in elementary and secondary schools with the usual incidents of complaints about school. There were days when they would ask her permission to skip school. She loved her children, and when they asked to do something much more interesting than going to school, she did not have the heart to refuse.

She said, "I hated school so much that in all honesty to myself I could not tell them that they had to go school." It was a question of being honest with herself. She had known a higher value than school as a child. She could not say, "No!"

She remembered when she was in school. She hated it. School did not have a long tradition in her society. Only toward the end of the nineteenth century had the first schools appeared on the prairies where the Lakota reservations had been established.

The first schools had a dual purpose. They educated the children to read, write and solve problems in arithmetic. They also learned how to keep house as white women did, if they were girls, or how to farm and do elementary carpentry when they were boys.

Somehow, the enthusiasm we often find in children today when they discover the wonders of kindergarten was not present in her life. That was because education had another purpose which she found distasteful. Education was cross-cultural; a member of one culture taught pupils of another culture. Often it was to train the children to take their place in the culture of the teacher. She was being educated to take her place in the white world. That world was not Lakota. She, a Lakota girl, was being educated to take her place in the world of the settlers who had come among her people. She was being educated to take her place in "white society."

She has done well. Today she manages a conference center where people gather for learning sessions and find a very comfortable setting for which she cares. The first objective of her education has been achieved. She is skilled in the arts of housekeeping and uses them effectively.

The other goal was the cause of her pain. She resisted the change in cultures that was forced upon her. At home she would have learned how to keep house as a Lakota woman. There would have been little difference in the two since a sense of neatness and organization would have been found in the Lakota as well as white traditions. However, since the white society had more items to use, she learned use and care of different cloths and clothing and the various instruments employed in their care. All that made her comfortable in Lakota society would have been there. The Lakotas' way of life had endured for more than twenty thousand years and was in no way failing to provide the setting for meeting her needs. It was a good life. It had endured comfortably for more than twenty millennia.

To look back that far in history is to see far beyond the Roman empire and the dynasties of Egypt. To read books about the life of the American Indians that were written a century ago is to encounter all the prejudices of even well meaning writers of that day toward Indian culture. They were convinced that it was their duty to "civilize" the Indian. It was their obligation to raise to a higher level of living all the underprivileged people of the earth.

But, were they underprivileged? They had developed schemes of life that worked. They had distinct cultures that met their demands of life. The turmoil of the industrial revolution, which brought so much misery to the English and other European people who embraced it, was not known to the Lakota people nor any of the tribal, non-European people of the world. That is not to say that the non-Europeans had an idyllic life. The harshness of existence was there. They did not have the benefits of developing medicine that wonderfully extends life. There were uneducated beliefs that placed a burden on tribal people. As we look around the world and see the development of societies, although not in the European way, we know that all of us live in a world that has fallen from the ideal life that can be envisioned. However, all the histories the of world reveal that none of us has found such an existence.

There is a theory that only by exploiting the new world of its gold and silver and moving it to Europe, was the financing of the industrial revolution possible. In Europe, as the theory goes, there was not sufficient material wealth to underwrite the financial costs of the industrial revolution. The high levels of life that the Mayan and Aztecs achieved in what is now Latin America was not appreciated for itself. Leaders were killed and nations were enslaved. The dominance of Europe could not be resisted. Europe was not alone. Asia and Africa, and even South and North America, were guilty of advances against other people. Slavery appeared in every continent. Human sacrifice was often the sacrifice of conquered neighbors who were not treated as neighbors, but as enemies.

It is possible that the Lakotas and other tribal people of America would have evolved into mercenary nations whose objective would have been to teach the rest of the earth their values. What seems clear is that no nation can establish itself as a master and expect to continue that domination of others. Egypt, Greece and Rome in ancient times were founded on systems of slavery. In this country we fought the tragic Civil War because of the institution of slavery in our midst. Even now we are not free of the intolerable institution of racism, one group possessing the deep belief that they are better somehow than men and women of other races.

We could laugh, if it were not so tragic. We look around our world today and see how the blinded wisdom of Europe has failed to lead the world's people to a happy, peaceful state.

The Lakota mother had not been able to insist that her children attend school every day. What had happened to her that she could talk about this now? She was ready to admit that she had a broader view now and was able to discuss this subject which had been for years a question of honesty to herself.

What had happened in her life was meeting a white woman who had, with great tact and patience, worked with her. This woman had spoken to me about her desire to be of help to the Lakota woman. I encouraged her and advised that she should use delicacy and great tact in this encounter. She should be very patient in meeting her, allow her to set the pace at which they would exchange ideas. She began by coming to the Lakota woman's home where she would be met at the door but not be invited inside. They talked and became friendly with each other. In time, she asked her to lunch in a restaurant where she would feel at ease. She talked about her children and shared with her the interest she had in her own children's welfare. Slowly she proved her worth as a mother and a confidant. I still recall, after months of meeting, the day she told me that she had been invited into the Lakota woman's house. She had been sincere; she had been patient; she had won the Lakota woman's confidence.

By that time they were friends. They shared confidences with each other. They were looking for answers that were solid. She had talked to her about the importance of education in the modern world. She understood the Lakota woman's hatred of school. She grasped how school for the Lakota woman was a separation from the traditions of her culture. She could sympathize with her and regret that she had to endure so painful an experience. But, she was able to impress upon her the importance of her children's education. Once she understood, she could appreciate how good it was for her children to attend school regularly. Then it became necessary for her to share her new insight with another person. I am fortunate that she came to tell me of the experience that changed her outlook on education.

A few years after she had met and talked with me about the education of her children, the occupation of Wounded Knee occured. Something similar to her experience with the white woman who became her friend seems to have happened to many of the young Indians of high school and college age. They began graduating from high school and going to college. Scholarships were available. Many of the prestigious universities offered free tuition in their graduate schools to members of minority groups. They accept and have become the professional members of Indian society. For the most part they have taken positions on reservations and in urban Indian communities. Some have gone on only for their own benefit, but that has always to be expected. This is not a perfect world.

When the Lakota people at Oglala, South Dakota formed Oyate to enable their children to be proud of their Lakota tradition, they had an intangible notion of what they desired. As their children responded to the education programs that Oyate produced, they gave the evidence in tangible form that the goal was being reached. As there was a group of children who exhibited this pride, that became a tangible characteristic of these Lakotas. With the individual child, it was an ideal. With the group of children, it was a structural institution.

The tradition of counting coup can be used as an example of how the Lakotas took an intangible and made it into a tangible ideal. Individuals sought to count coup and reduced it from an intangible factor in their lives to a tangible ideal that they were able to carry out. Because so many were able to achieve this quality of life, it became an institution of their culture. They grew up with the expectation of this quality in their lives. But not all Lakota men set out as young men to achieve the skill of counting coup. That did not mean they were not Lakotas. They had other skills which they developed. They may have developed the skill of working with porcupine quills, the traditional art form of the Lakotas. They would pluck the quills and soak them in water. When they were soft, they would braid them dyed with colors that accented their dress made from the hides of animals. Each member had distinct talents. No one had a talent to do everything well.

A deeper look into the nature of culture will reveal that not all the intangibles are good. There are characteristics that are not desirable for people of any culture. Despair is such a characteristic. Anger, jealousy impatience can also be included in the Center of Intangibles. They do not produce cultural elements that are desirable in any society.

In the Lakota culture, since its members were placed on reservations, despair has been a notable characteristic of the men who belong to that culture. Most modern Americans have no idea of how the Indian man found his life useless once he was a prisoner on the reservation. Yet, it was not the reservation that provided such emptiness in his life. Anywhere he might have been, he would have felt useless. He could no longer embrace the ideal of the warrior-hunter. They were forcibly restricted to the reservations unable to count coup, unable to hunt buffalo.

The memory of Custer's defeat made those who assumed responsibility for American Indians to be wary of their movements away from their home reservation.

It does not seem possible that Indian agents grasped what a devastating blow that restriction to a reservation, a parcel of land, was for these warriors of the plains, masterful horsemen who had caught the imagination of the world. Sometimes tribes shared their reservations with another tribe, occasionally a former enemy. Agents realized that the Indians lived by hunting, but never seemed to comprehend how deeply that quality reached into their being. They assumed that they were not "civilized" and that all their characteristics came from the wild state into which they were born. That Indians had deep feelings of identity, just as members of other cultures do, did not enter their reasoning process.

The Indians were civilized. Their culture manifested that civilization in a different way. When we look around us and find such incredible rates of crime, can we hold our culture up as an example of civilized society? When it is sometimes suggested that "greed" should be the motivating force in our lives and that a complete disregard of other members of our society should characterize us, can we say that is civilized. Indians as tribal people always had a concern about the members of their tribe. What is civilization, if not a concern about the welfare of one's fellows?

Recent stories about Indians have dealt with that very point, that Indians had feelings just as early setters did. Indian mothers mourned the death of their husbands and sons. They would cut off the tips of their fingers and slash their arms. They would forever carry signs of their losses on their bodies.

When the right to hunt and go on the warpath were denied the Indian men, sociologically they had no reason to live. That despair swept through the succeeding generations of boys as they came to the junior high school. They learned from the men who were elders in their society. They looked around and they saw no purpose in life. They were youths with ambition but had no where to go. The more gifted an individual was, the less hope he had for his future.

Their response to the call for forest fire fighters can be easily understood as it provided one last opportunity to be a real Indian man. Likewise the enlistment of Indian men in the armed forces when this country went to war, was another opportunity for Indian men to face some of the daring challenges of their forefathers. It was not the old Indian form of war, but the word was the same and they responded to it.

In the normal course of events today it is usually the husband who will do the speaking first when a couple comes to discuss a problem that the couple is having in their marriage, in their desire to purchase a home, in any situation that involves the two of them. Before the occupation of Wounded Knee in 1973 nine times out of ten when an Indian couple came to discuss a problem, the wife did the talking and only later would the husband make a remark. Sometimes he never said a word. He despaired of his position in society. Even to this day many Indian men have that sense of despair running through their lives. Alcoholism is so frequently their escape from this sense of inadequacy in the modern world.

For a non-Indian teacher in an Indian school, the problem of junior high boys turning to alcohol can be difficult to grasp until he understands the devastation that the Indian men suffered and that has been passed down generation by generation by those who teach the Indian boys their way of living. They see those who drink steadily. They are assured that Indian men drink. In fact older men who drink, and have died from alcoholism, have told me, while alive, that it is a quality of the Indian man to drink heavily.

The more talented an Indian boy is, the more heavily he will drink. The more desperately he will feel deep inside himself how hopeless his life must be. This is not to say that less talented youths will feel less attraction to alcohol. For a society that had not developed the use of alcohol for 20,000 or more years, this is a tragic situation.

Now they can leave the reservation, but there are no longer huge herds of buffalo to hunt across the stretches of prairie that reach to the horizon. They have no way of behaving like Indian warriors of old. Alcohol had been introduced to them, and they used it as a means of escape.

However, as has been indicated above there are many who now find their challenge in education and have gone on to earn degrees from colleges and universities. Yet on the college campus there is so frequently a growing search for alcohol and the relief from stress that it imparts. Here there is also a larger percentage of women who are graduating with the men. Among the Lakota people women are frequently among the leaders in Indian activities. But, Indian men are taking their place.

That was not always the case. When men were reluctant to speak, women were the aggressors. One of the historical movements in this country was that led by Ada Deer, a friend of mine for many years and who was the Assistant Secretary for Indian Affairs in the Department of the Interior. She led the Menominee Indians of Wisconsin in their struggle to regain for their tribe reservation status with all the benefits that federal recognition includes. The loss of reservation status for her tribe was an outrage that she would not accept. With some other women, she organized the terminated people of her tribe. The reservation had been terminated from federal recognition and had been turned into a county in Wisconsin.

She and her crew lobbied Congress so effectively that the reservation's terminated status was reversed. It became their land again. The county became again the Menominee Indian Reservation; they had federal recognition and they had the benefits that the Bureau of Indian Affairs and the Indian Health Service can provide. The Menominee women succeeded in their battle with the federal government, as Ada Deer signed on April 22, 1975 with Secretary of the Interior Morton a deed that conveyed back into trust status the reservation of the Menominee tribe.

Their success aroused some resentment from the young men of the Menominee tribe. They noted what Ada Deer and the women had done. They were desperate to be Indian men who acted when they saw the need to do something. They organized the Menominiee Warriors Society. On January 1, 1975, New Years's Day, the Warrior Society took over the abandoned noviate of the Alexian Brothers, a Catholic Religious Community dedicated to the care of the sick and elderly, at Gresham, Wisconsin near the Menominee land. The seizure was an indication of the rivalry that had developed between the dedicated women and the men who were trying so desperately to regain status in their tribe. It is to the credit of Ada Deer that once the reservation was restored and functioning with the Bureau of Indian Affairs that she left the administration of the tribe. She knew she had done her job and that the turmoil in the tribe could be settled without her.

Just the mention of "reservations" is bound to bring remarks that Indians are better off without reservations. Some argue that reservations are sites of poverty and degradation that provide no opportunity for Indians and that the United States would be better off with every reservation in his country terminated as the federal government during the administration of Dwight Eisenhower had begun to do. Certainly the Menominee Indians would not agree.

Ada Deer is their modern hero.

Certainly such arguments have some value, but the destruction of all reservations would have a much more disastrous effect on American Indians. Such reasoning has some of the misguided thought that has resulted in such division of Indians and non-Indians in this country. The reservations have become homes to America's Indians. They are no longer prisoners in their own land. Over half of the Indian population now lives in urban areas. California, of all the states, has the largest number of Indians living there. Indians look to the reservations as their homes. As Americans of European descent look to their nations of origin in Europe, so Indians look to their reservations. Imagine telling the Irish that they can not go "home" to Ireland again!

Mention has been made above on how the United States was founded for white, European setters, not Indians. When the United States was founded, there was discussion of including American Indians as citizens. There was talk of having an Indian state with Indian representation in Congress, but it was not accepted by those who founded the United States. The United States began with no Indians as citizens. Indians had tribal citizenship, although they did not use the term "citizenship" in their tribes or nations which were far older than the United States.

As Indians did not need the United States before it was founded, they were not needed once it was established. They were the people who owned the land that became the United States. That is their uniqueness. It can never be denied them. They owned this land. Even the Osage people in Oklahoma who became rich when oil was discovered on their reservation owned part of this country although not the portion that became the Osage Reservation in Oklahoma.

Frequently the United States is accused of placing Indians on the worst land in the country. What is meant by "the worst land" is usually land that could not be farmed. That is true, but I have been told by Lakotas that "we were not farmers. We did not want to farm." That also is true, but the federal government spent a lot of money trying to turn Indians into farmers. The Indians knew what they wanted but had no voice to make that choice known.

Once the buffalo herds were decimated, and the Lakotas were placed securely on the reservations with no opportunity to escape, the federal government made a logical move. It provided cows for the Indians and allowed the Indians to become cowboys. It almost worked. It was a natural move, but hardly anyone who is not Indian remembers it.

The land was allotted to the various heads of households. Each had his own land and was given his own cattle. But the sense of community was too strong in the Indians to operate as individual ranchers. They operated in common and disregarded the boundary lines of the government's allotments. They had never believed that man could own the earth, their mother. At the end of the nineteenth century and into the 1920's they became the ranchers of the west. They were successful. They ran large herds of cattle in war and peace. If they had been allowed to continue, there would be a different story today of the American Indians. They were masterful horsemen. To become cowboys was the right thing for Indians of the prairies. They would not be fighting enemy tribes, but they would use the same technique to run their herds.

During the first World War, when an exceptionally large number of Indians who were not citizens of the United States volunteered to fight with its forces abroad, the change began to take place. It was at that time that the Lakotas needed a leader, a man who could look ahead and make the right decisions for the people. They did not find a leader. They had no voice in government to improve their status.

As the war began, the price of wheat began to increase. Then it skyrocketed. Even land on Indian reservations could make a profit if sown in wheat for such prices. Wheat farmers beseeched the Bureau of Indian Affairs for the right to lease the Indian land on the reservations and raise wheat. It was here that leadership was needed. They needed somebody who could look ahead and make the right decision. Superintendents of reservations in the Bureau of Indian Affairs were told by Washington authorities to allow the wheat growers to lease the land. So the land was leased.

The Indians leased the land and had checks coming to them as they sold the cattle. "We didn't sell cattle by the carload; we sold them by the trainload," a long deceased Indian told me. For a time all went well. Leasing land for wheat was profitable. Then came the agricultural depression of the early twenties. No one could make money growing wheat on Indian land. The leases were worthless. The cattle were gone. The land needed years to return to the state in which it could support herds of cattle again. The Indians suffered a psychological blow that some experts claim was as severe as the establishment of reservations. The Lakota men were again without a meaningful role to play. The Lakota world was destitute.

The federal government began a program of gardening and built canning factories, small structures where a community had facilities for canning the produce it raised in the gardens. The Boss Farmer became an important person in reservation life. He was a government employee who had some expertise in farming. He guided the Indians in their planting, growing and harvesting of crops. By the end of the second World War the canning factories stood empty or served as homes for impoverished families.

With the second World War, the roads opened into the outside world. War time jobs were available, thousands of men and women went into the service. Others went to work in defense factories. The world of the Lakotas would never be the same. They had begun to live off the reservations. Never again would they have the whole community living together.

The transistor radio became a reality in the Lakota world. The pavement of roads on reservations allowed the Lakotas to enter the outside world very easily and at the same time allowed the outside world to enter the reservations of this broad country. Then the federal government began its program of relocating Indians in the large American cities. So many Lakotas were moved to California that a sociology professor from one of the universities there came back to the reservation doing research on a book about the homeland of the Indians who had moved to California.

Should the Indian reservations be destroyed? Should that land become just a part of the United States? I do not think so. Only if one were not concerned with the culture of the Indian people, would it be possible to terminate the reservations. Even though many no longer live on the reservations, their homeland is their reservation. As the Irish can not give up Galway Bay, Indians can not forget the reservations. They may live away from their reservations, but it is home. It is where they are buried when they die. "I want to be buried with my people," is the refrain one often hears. They will live in America's cities, but they want to be buried among their own.

Possibly, the children who have been born away form the reservations and who only visit them from time to time will not feel so strongly about the reservations. Moreover, there are many who still live on the reservations and feel that this is a place from which their people come. It is culture showing itself in the lives of the Indians. One might as well tell them it no longer exists as to tell the Irish that Ireland is English.

THE NEED FOR CULTURAL IDENTITY

— CHAPTER XI—

The lingual corruption of names for American Indians is often overlooked by the average United States' citizen. They look upon the words such as Sioux and Chippewa as age old names for various tribes that have existed in this country. The word Sioux is a French corruption of the Chippewa word for enemy. The word Chippewa is a French corruption of the Ottawa word for enemy. The French settlers as they moved west adjusted to their tongue the word for enemy of the tribe they were leaving. The Indians were in no position to correct the error, nor were any other groups of people in the area. These names have become part of the English language when speaking of the tribes who have so been renamed.

The Chippewa and the Sioux have become adjusted to the erroneous names and among themselves use their original names since they are a group of tribes with dialectical differences in language. The Lakota, Nakota and Dakota are related, but do not have identical languages. The Lakotas do not have a "d" sound in their language. The Dakotas do not have a "1" sound in their language. The Nakotas have both "d" and "1" sounds in their language. If a person has a knowledge of one language, he is able to understand the spoken language of the other tribes. Today the word "Sioux" unites these three tribes who had no

Indian word to indicate that union. As the Dakotas live to the east in Minnesota and eastern South Dakota, they were the first Sioux to be contacted. Just west of them are the Nakota tribe and in western South Dakota is the largest tribe of the three, the Lakotas. As the settlers moved westward they encountered the Dakota first, and so today there is North and South Dakota. Had the settlers come from the west, we should probably had North and South Lakota. As the settlers began to learn that they were three distinct tribes, they often used the word "Dakota" for the whole group. The Indians knew it was not correct and referred to themselves as the Dakota, Nakota and Lakota. Those words may not be familiar to the average American ear, but they are signs of their identity to members of the three tribes.

It is not surprising to have so few residents of this country have a very inadequate knowledge of American Indians. Our schools do not teach clearly the status of Indians. There should be emphasis on the three governments in this country, the federal, the state and the tribal governments. Somehow tribal government never comes across as a real government, but it is. There is not enough emphasis on Indians having the only dual citizenship in accord with the laws of this land. Even the President of the United States, Ronald Reagan, while he was in office seemed to grasp at the identity of Indians when he was answering a question about them while visiting the former Soviet Union when he spoke about the Osage Indians of Oklahoma having oil on their land. He gave the impression that all Indians have oil when not all Osage Indians have oil wells.

Curiously because there was money involved in this case, the constitution of the Osage Tribe included only those who had a head right to the oil, that is those who had a right to take oil from the oil wells for their personal benefit. Because the Osage were a generous people, even some individuals who were not Osage but who had head rights were allowed membership in the Osage Tribe. In the early 1990's a tribal constitution that includes all Osage tribal members was accepted, but for years prior to this change many meetings were held on this development. Many of them in Washington, D.C. at their Senators offices where I frequently was a participant.

Similarly when the Alaska Native land settlement legislature was under consideration in Washington, native corporations worth millions of dollars were established. Members of the board of directors were one day made members, while only the day before they had been busy hunting walrus in the Bering Sea. Apparently because of the money involved, these corporations were set up after the model of a business corporation, not a tribal organization. A time limit of twenty years was established for the corporations to make a profit. After that time the Alaska land that was included in the wealth of the corporation was subject to the usual rules of business. It could be taken from the corporation if the corporation was in debt and had no way of paying off that obligation. Since the Alaska natives are more inclined to traditional subsistence hunting, fishing and food gathering which includes harvesting of berries and wild plants, than any other native tribe in this country, the loss of that land was a considerable threat to those tribes that did go bankrupt. Only enactment of legislation several years before the termination of the time limit established by the original legislation prevented this threat to the Indians, Eskimos and Aleuts of Alaska.

The inability of members of Congress to understand the details of subsistence hunting, fishing and food gathering were clearly evident in this issue. Undoubtedly, there was some intention to have Alaska natives face the reality of business life, but there was no real grasp of how the tribes or villages, as they are known in Alaska, depend on subsistence fishing, hunting and food gathering to live. The solution of the business world were too sudden for many Alaska native people.

It should be noted that many of these Alaska native corporations have made real financial progress and are not in danger of collapse. Some of them, however, did need assistance.

Cases decided by the United States Supreme Court have recognized the right to subsistence fishing and hunting and food gathering. Alaska is a large area, and the few people living there are in the large cities. However, if Alaska were divided in two, it would make two states both considerably larger than Texas. Alaska has far more land than people.

The state in recent years established the Alaska Natives Commission which has brought out its three volume report this past year. It is interesting to note some observations by Dr. Robert Alberts, a psychiatrist in private practice and a member of the Advisory Council of the Alaska Native Foundation. He writes, "It was difficult for me, in those early days, to understand why there was so much frustration, anger and violence among the people in the villages. For these were people abundantly capable of support and genuine friendship and so free of prejudice toward others. It took time to develop insight into the sickness which had spread through the Native communities and which was causing so much self-destructive behavior, especially among the young people....

"Mental health is the positive attitude toward life, together with the skills to cope successfully with life's stresses, which make it possible for us to reach our highest potential as human beings. Our coping skills are important to help us maintain a state of well-being. Equally important are an understanding of the stresses we encounter in life and the support we receive from our support systems: our families, friends and communities that we belong to....

"Looking back on the recent history of Alaska, it appears that many of the problems of today are related to the attitude of the non-Alaska caregivers who came to the state in great numbers to 'save' the Native people. With some exceptions, these outsiders were thoroughly convinced - as is typical of members of most dominant societies - about the superiority and rightness of their own culture. Due in part to ignorance and cultural nearsightedness, they believed that replacing the Native culture with their own was beneficial and therefore justified.

"Before the newcomers came to Alaska the Native people were not in need of salvation. For many centuries their cultural traditions and their knowledge had provided them with the skills to survive successfully in their own environment. The disintegration started when non-Native culture, totally foreign to the natural environment of Alaska, caused great disruption between the land and the Native people...."

After the Native way of life became increasingly influenced by their dominant culture and society, the Native people themselves either by choice or by coercion - became dependent on the outside world. This dependency, which is the single most damaging force with respect to Natives' self-esteem, gives the artificially created situation its life by means of scores of federal, state and private agencies that are still the business of "saving" the Natives.

"...Natives cannot help but observe that with each new arrival of every new service and each new non-Native provider, comes more damage to the Native way of life and to the pride and independence of the people.

"The unwillingness on the part of many non-Native providers to give up control, has left Native people unprepared for the changes which have taken place. It continues to foster a state of dependency that destroys the self-esteem of the people who find themselves caught between two worlds." How apt the line from Matthew Arnold's poem "Stanzas from the Grand Chartreuse,"

"Wandering between two worlds, one dead, The other powerless to be born."

The very nature of a person cries out for identity with the culture into which he or she has been born. We do not realize how important culture is to a person. We never see it. It begins with intangibles. We begin learning it before we are able to talk. We have people move into our world and begin to take this culture from us, leaves us with a sense of inadequacy. Our life has been taken from us. People who did not know how we lived have tried to impose a scheme of life upon us and we know it does not work. We are confused. We do not have the guide lines by which to chose. An interruption in our scheme of life has been made and we are not able to see the scheme, the plan, the pattern the structure for our life. Something maddening has entered our existence. We are driven to drink, to long, intoxicated drink where we begin to think that in intoxication we have the way to life. Drunkenness is the scheme of life.

An inmate at Wildwood Correctional Center serving twenty years for murder told the commission, "Basically where it all comes from is the family. Before I got incarcerated, I was raised in a family that was dysfunctional, where there were drugs and alcohol, and where there was abuse... I think we should do Native counseling in the villages." He recognizes the need children have to be trained, to be shown, to be guided into their roles.

From my own experience with the Lakota people I have conversed with families about the problems of dysfunctional families and the benefits that counseling can provide. When alcohol and drugs have removed all functions from a family, counseling can provide a view of what is necessary for a meaningful life. A mother told me that she had to raise a family before she learned how to teach the children.

Dr. Alberts concludes, "Only after hope has been restored and depression has lifted can people become aware of their own strengths and the spiritual strength of their cultural tradition. The thought that cultural traditions retard development is totally wrong. As long as a culture remains alive and can incorporate new ideas while remaining true to its basic spiritual foundation, development and progress can become living realities.

"...The true nature of the sickness which has spread throughout the Native villages is the state of dependency which led to the loss of direction and self-esteem....

"The healing will have to come from within the Native community. And it will have to come by means of the re-awakening of the independence, the pride and the sense of purpose which at one time guided the people in their journey through the centuries."

What Dr. Alberts says to the Native people of Alaska can be said in retrospect of all the Native people who have suddenly found themselves invaded by other people, bound to the notion that they have to civilize them regardless of the burden it puts upon themselves.

When we recall the Lakota woman who felt guilty about insisting that her children should go to school, or the community at Oglala who had the insight to teach their children traditions of Lakota culture in school before the tribe took away their funding for that project, or those who came clamoring to Wounded Knee in 1973 and waved an American flag upside down as a sign of distress, we can seed the validity of his words. Culture is a way of living that is taught informally to children by the elders of the community.

Not only in the Americas, but through Asia and the Pacific, Africa and Australia, Europe with its centuries of wars, South America as well as North America we have seen the conflict in cultures that makes native people confused in their own world and forced to abandon their culture for that which a foreigner has brought in the name of their civilization.

The report says, "...(T)here can be little doubt that an entire population is at risk. At risk of becoming permanently imprisoned in America's under-class, mired in both the physical and spiritual poverty that accompany such social standing. At risk of leading lives, generation to generation, characterized by violence, alcohol abuse and cycles of personal and social destruction. At risk of losing, irretrievably, cultural strengths and attributes essential to the building of a new and workable social and economic order. And at risk, inevitably, of permanently losing the capacity to self-esteem - the capacity to make considered and appropriate decisions about how life in Native communities should be lived "

While this is written about the Natives of Alaska, it can be written of all native people. In Alaska we have the last American frontier which sweeps across the vast tundra of that land, across the rugged, snow covered mountains, across rivers that freeze solid in winter only to burst their frozen barriers as Spring touches their solid wraps and turns them into gushing water ways, across the low lands where rivers twist interminably back and forth so what is a short distance by plane becomes miles longer when the water flows and people travel in native boats, across the many river fishing camps where people gather fish for the coming season when snow will cover the land and across the vast Bering Sea where whales erupt from the waves and shoot toward the stars, where walruses and seals dive and play. Across this land native people have experienced the shock and stress that settlers brought who had no comprehension of the damage they were doing to native people because they sought to civilize them.

The natives were civilized! They knew the depths of love and affection. They knew the thrill of victory in battle and hunting. They had tales to recite in epic form. Their art forms spread with incredible delicacy over leather clothing and walrus tusks.

112

Their way of life was different and so it was considered wrong. Their ways were contrary to those of the settlers and were considered uncivilized.

The Federation of Natives in the Final Report of the Alaska Natives Commission is quoted, "For many Natives, the sense of personal, familial and cultural identity that is a prerequisite to healthy and productive life is being lost in a haze of alcohol induced despair that not infrequently results in violence perpetrated upon self and family."

As a state, Alaska has probably the strongest determination to remake the native people along their own tradition although they came as settlers to that state. So much needs to be done to free the natives from the confusion in which they now exist. They have snowmobiles and transistor radios. Some go to college and receive an education. But, older people are not free to subsist on fishing and hunting and gathering of wild berries and plants. They have won in court the right to their traditional way of subsistence.

The other states are not without blame in their treatment of native people, the American Indians. They live so close to them that the Indian's image is not shaded into a romantic notion as it would be when viewed over distances of thousands of miles. Some tribes, especially the Mashantucket Pequot in Connecticut, have found an economic boost in gaming casinos. They have a greater income than Donald Trump's Taj Mahal in Atlantic City. With the increased monetary gain that gambling brings, they now have an authority they never knew. Money speaks. Some Indians are making money and it is speaking. Strangely enough it may provide a means of self-esteem for the Indians, but there is always the resentment that the descendants of settlers have against them. Where do we find the love for our fellow man if everything he tries is held against him? And most Indians do not have gaming casinos, but who will recognize that when emotions lessen his reasoning powers?

Money was the cause of Indians going into the gaming business. In California the Cabazons, a small band of Indians, noticed what was happening in that state. Around the area card rooms were in operation. They decided to open a similar card room, but with this one decisive distinction; its profits would go to the tribe with no tax going to the state. The State of California objected. All gaming profits were to be taxed by its treasury. A suit was brought by California against the Cabazon Indians. It went all the way to the United States Supreme Court for a decision. In 1987 the court ruled that the Cabazons had the right to self-government which included absolute control of its gaming operations. From that recognition of tribal sovereignty and its control over gaming projects in states which allow elsewhere in the state the same gaming that Indian tribes offer has sprung the phenomenon of Indian Gaming. Because this kind of gaming makes very large amounts of money, states and individual persons are suspect of it. However, if we are to be true to our cause of civilizing the Indian, recognizing their right to gaming revenues is part of our civilizing actions. So much of the old ways are gone with the wind, it is time for them to handle money as modern businessmen.

In so many places of the lower forty eight states the passing years have seen a steady erosion of tradition, a wasting of culture. So much of a way of life has gone that can never be brought back. Where tribes have income it is best for them to take charge of their own lives and put together at least a semblance of their traditions. It will never be the old way of life, but it will be theirs with dances and dress and hopefully some of their traditional values such as wisdom, generosity, reverence and courage. Many are going to college now. They are being trained. Americans for Indian Opportunity is running a program each year in which twenty-two Indians gather periodically through the year in Washington and Albuquerque and other places learning to heal their needs and to establish a union among themselves. Tribes can no longer exist in isolation. They need to join each other to provide support and strength where they are needed. The age of Internet is upon us and the Indians will be apart of it.

As Wendell Chino, for many years President of the Mescalero Apache Tribe, said in an address to the New Mexico legislature in Santa Fe on racetracks being driven out of business by Casino gambling, "When Wal-Mart comes in, there is no subsidy for the small businessman who gets wiped out. So maybe we are limiting our subsidies too much."

He concluded, "Indians have never had a level playing field. We have always been underdogs. We have always fought for our lands. We have always fought for our communities. Maybe, some day we will be on parity." He is an Indian of this modern age. He knows where he comes form. He recognizes the cultural tradition of his people. He is an Indian but he recognizes he can fit into the modern world. He has something to teach the young members of his community.

As Indians have become attorneys and now look to the intricacies of law for the protection of tribal rights which treaties have guaranteed to individual tribes, so other Indians have prepared themselves for varied aspects of tribal manifestation. They are artists and Certified Public Accountants, although one would hardly expect expertise in that field an accomplishment of Indian students. However, a people dominated by the right hemisphere of the brain can produce CPA's as easily as a people dominated by the left hemisphere of the brain can produce artists. Not all members of any population group are dominated by the same hemisphere of the brain. Some are dominated by the other hemisphere.

The War on Poverty in Lydon Johnson's presidency had an effect in American Indian and Alaska Native communities that is not often recognized. It had programs that reached down to where poverty existed and made efforts to bring about changes. The administrations that succeeded Johnson for political reasons removed almost all the structures that were erected in his presidency. What they sought was elimination of the people in poverty rising as a political power to confront the established powers of the nation. Certainly, many of the people who served on boards of directors in the War on Poverty were enabled by the confidence in themselves that they received in such service to work for better jobs and positions in the communities where they lived. It would have been better had succeeding generations had the same opportunities.

CALL THEM SIOUX

— CHAPTER XII —

The corruption of tribal names which the French explorers have left us has taken root deep within our knowledge of the Indian world. They have become registered in legal titles in the various states of this nation. "The United Sioux Tribes" is an organization that works for the benefit of all the Sioux tribes that exist in South Dakota. The very word, Sioux, reaches beyond the limits of Sioux tribes to tribes that are in some way related to the Sioux. It has meaning in the United States Census of 1990 where a footnote states "Any entry with the spelling 'Siouan' was miscoded to Sioux in North Carolina". What that means is that the tribes linguistically related to the Sioux such as the Crow, Catawba, Winnebago, Iowa, Osage or other related tribes were classified as Sioux in the census taken in North Carolina. Indians were counted, but not given their specifically tribal name. It should not be assumed that there are few Indians left in North Carolina because it has an Indian population that ranks in the top ten among the states. Here a large portion of the Indians do not belong to federally recognized tribes but are nonetheless Indian. Moreover, the Sioux were first recognized in this state when the settlers came from Europe. They moved to the Dakotas where they now have their home reservations.

The Catawbas, who remained mostly in South Carolina and have recently come to a legal conclusion with the federal, state and county governments granting them a portion of land and a large amount of money for the 144,000 acres of land that was illegally taken from them under a treaty signed with the British before the establishment of the United States, are linguistic relatives of the Sioux but are not called Sioux.

The non-Indian population of this country finds it easier to combine the Lakota, the Nakota and the Dakota into one group and call them Sioux. However, among the Sioux there is now a greater effort to call themselves by their ancient names, such as Lakota. That is what their ancestors were called, and that is what they prefer to be called. That is who they are.

The fact that most non-Indians find it difficult to remember their tribal names does not count with them. They have a point. When citizens of this land spend a considerable amount of money and time to trace their own ancestry so that they may know who they are, they can at least grant their Indian neighbors the courtesy of knowing who they are.

While we are Americans, or citizens of the United States, each of us has a history that reaches into foreign lands. Either we, or more likely our predecessors, renounced the ruler and the country which they left to seek the benefits of living in the United States. Each of us has become a citizen of the United States, but the Indians did not go through such a process. They are first of all Lakota or Navajo or Mohawk or some other tribe. It is from them that the land on which the United States rests was purchased in most cases by treaty with that individual tribe. When the United States was founded, they were not granted citizenship but were mentioned in the Constitution of the United States of America as outsiders with whom this country related.

In Article One, Section Two of the Constitution when representation and taxation are mentioned, the phrase "and excluding Indians not taxed" appears. That is a recognition of them as persons, but not as citizens of the United States. Moreover, unless one is a citizen, no tax is normally levied against that person, and so no taxation of Indians is intended.

In the same article under Section Seven is the commerce clause. The U. S. Congress is "to regulate Commerce with foreign Nations, and among the several States, and with the Indian Tribes; ...." Indian tribes are placed on a par with the several states and foreign nations. Later when Chief Justice John Marshall was struggling with an exact description of Indian tribes, he referred to them in Cherokee Nation v. Georgia as "dependent, domestic nations". They were "dependent" because the United States had taken away their right to engage in international affairs. They were "domestic" because the United States recognized them as members or citizens of tribes or nations residing within the boundaries of the United States. No other population group in this country has that recognition. As immigrants from foreign countries became citizens of the United States, they

117

renounce their former ruler and country. Indians never had to renounce their membership or citizenship in their native tribes. In this situation there is no difference between citizens and members of a tribe. The words can be interchanged as the word "citizen" came to this country with the European settlers and the word "member" was used to describe the individual Indian's participation in the structure and unity of his government.

Nations do not pay taxes. They collect taxes. So it is not surprising that tribal members, as citizens of tribes who are governments, living on tribal land do not pay state taxes. However, when they purchase items off the reservation, individual tribal members pay all the taxes that other residents pay. Or if they live off the reservation they are subjected to all the taxes that their neighbors pay, income taxes, sales taxes, land taxes and all the other forms of taxes everyone has to pay.

Tribes have their own government and elect members to their tribal councils as well as tribal President and other executive offices. As was noted above, they are also citizens of the United States. The have dual citizenship.

They are citizens or members of their tribes whose existence antedates the existence of the United States. They were named citizens of the United States by Congressional legislation in 1924. Earlier laws had recognized Indians as citizens if they in effect abandoned their tribe. That began with the Dawes General Allotment Act in 1887.

In 1924 when all Indians, by the fact that they were Indians, became citizens of the United States, Congress made no demands to require them, as the federal law requires of immigrants who seek United States citizenship, to renounce their head of state and the country he rules. The fact that Indians are unique in their right to dual citizenship is evident from this history of Indians in relationship to the United States.

The only other person, who has dual citizenship in another nation as well as the United States at the same time and whose citizenship is recognized by the United States as well as that foreign nation, is a person like the late Princess Grace Kelly Rainier of Monaco or someone who is so singularly honored. It is greatly significant that Indians have dual citizenship. No other population group has been granted such a distinction. So when there is a reference that in the United States all people are equal, in regard to the Indians their is not a possibility of their equality being the same as all other citizens. The fact that they are Indian, grants them automatically a difference. U. S. citizens of Chinese, French, Brazilian, Egyptian or any foreign descent can never claim the relationship to the United States that Indians claim. They never gave most of their homelands to the United States in treaties that "are the supreme law of the land."

The relationship of the United States to their Indians citizens deviates from the general rule of nations to their citizens. It is an anomaly. It began when Great Britain signed treaties with the tribes or nations living in the eastern part of the United States as they began the colonization of North America. It should be noted that the interchange of the term "tribe" with the term "nation" results from the culture of vastly different populations. A tribe is a group of persons who govern themselves and work in cooperation with one another. They are sovereign. From the European structure of society groups of people who are sovereign are referred to as a nation. Thus, there is the German nation, the Japanese nations, the Egyptian nation and all the nations of the world. However, a glance at Africa will turn up again the term "tribe". There is, for example, the Zulu tribe. It could be called the Zulu nation, but because the Zulus live in close cooperation with each other and do not have an elaborate, bureaucratic government, the term "tribe" is used. Whichever is used, the meaning is the same. They are a sovereign people. They govern themselves. They enter into agreements or sign treaties with foreign nations. "Tribe" and "nation" are interchangeable. As Europe colonized both North and South America, they encountered Indian groups with differences in the their structures of governments. Often the more elaborate governments were accompanied by more durable cities. These were frequently referred to as "nations". Thus in the south of what is now the United States and in Central and South America where Indians established permanent cities and more elaborate governments they are called nations. There are the Aztec nation and the Mayan nation. Whether the population group was called a "nation" or a "tribe", they were both sovereign. They governed themselves.

The remarkable part in this history is that once the United States of America was established, it continued to recognize the sovereignty of Indian nations. While the Indian tribes could no longer enter into treaties with Canada or Spain, they continued to have the right to govern themselves. This may be a limited form of sovereignty, but it is sovereignty. It is to the credit of the United States that it gave this recognition to the Indian tribes. It could have easily ignored then as most of the conquered tribal people experienced. As we look at the refugees of the world today, wandering as refugees across the world, we see the intolerance of nations toward one another.

From the time the United States was established until 1871 the treaty process was used in reaching agreement with the Indian tribes. The United States recognized them as "dependent, domestic nations" and employed the process of making treaties with them in working out the differences that existed between them.

Article Six of the Constitution describes its treaty making process as follows:

"This Constitution, and the Laws of the United States which shall be made in Pursuance thereof; and all the Treaties made, or which shall be made, under the Authority of the United States, shall be THE SUPREME LAW OF THE LAND; and the Judges in every State shall be bound thereby, any Thing in the Constitution or Laws of any State to the contrary notwithstanding." (Capitalized words were added by the author.)

The phrase which describes the importance of treaties is that they are "the supreme Law of the Land". Supreme means that it is of the highest rank or standing. Even should something be found in the Constitution itself or in the laws of the states, that would not be effective in limiting the force of treaties agreed to by both parties. The United States took on itself the responsibility of carrying out those treaties which the European powers made with Indian tribes prior to its establishment. Treaties are a highly serious form of law. They are nothing that one would handle very lightly and still be considered a citizen of the United States.

Our government is founded on treaties which we still sign today, but not with Indian tribes.

In 1871 the House of Representatives voiced its opinion that it should have more decision power in the disposition of Indian affairs. By law the treaties would be signed with the "advice and consent" of the Senate. No action by the House of Representatives was required. Through the latter part of the eighteenth century and most of the nineteenth century the Senate handled all the Indian issues that came along. The Senate was the Congressional division that handled treaties according to the Constitution. Then the House of Representatives began to think that since it was the house that originated the bills of taxation, it should have something to say about the payments that were so frequently a part of treaties. The government wanted more and more land and so had to make more and more payments to the tribes who lost their hunting land. In an obscure rider to the appropriation bill of 1871 Congress legislated that henceforth no treaties with Indian tribes would be allowed but all the provision of prior treaties with Indian tribes would remain in force.

The fact that the United States has so much to say about the status of Indian tribes is not taken lightly by American Indians. They recognize that they have an advantage over the other fourth world nations, that is nations which are included in a recognized, established nation, but they resent the interference in their lives. In some instances the United States Supreme Court hands down decisions that are of vital concern to them, but the only refuge they have is to appeal to Congress to pass a law which would negate the effect of the Supreme Court decision. This has happened a number of times, but there are other instances in which Congress has not acted to overrule the effect of a Supreme Court decision.

The longest case before the United States Supreme Court is an Indian case. The Sioux Tribe, to use the name the settlers gave to them, sued the federal government for a violation of the Treaty of 1868. In 1989 a decision was handed down that read in part, "A more ripe and rank case of dishonorable dealing will never, in all probability, be found in our history." The Court continued: When Congress passed the Act of 1877, there "was a breach of this nation's solemn obligation to reserve the Black Hills in perpetuity for occupation by the Indians." When the Hills were taken, the result was "a taking of tribal property, property which had been set aside for the exclusive occupation of the Sioux by the Fort Laramie Treaty of 1868." The Court went on to criticize "President Grant's duplicity in breaching the government's treaty obligation to keep trespassers out of the Black Hills."

The cause of this case was the discovery in 1874 of gold in the Black Hills by General George A. Custer, the impetuous commander who two years later would lead his entire cavalry unit to death at the Battle of the Little Big Horn River in Montana. After word of this discovery began circulating, gold miners rushed to the Black Hills to start digging for gold. The Black Hills were part of the reservation that was for the use of the Sioux. But who would stop white Americans from overrunning the land?

The United States sent the Indian Peace Commission to the Sioux to seek a revision of the 1868 treaty that gave them that territory. According to the wording of that treaty three fourths of the male population of the Indians occupying that land had to sign the new agreement. The Indians did not speak or write English and so used an X mark to indicate their approval. The Indian Peace Commission found a few who were willing to sign, but it is seriously doubted that they found three fourths of the men ready to mark their X against which a white man would write the individual Indian's name.

The names read Little Fox, Left Hand Bull, Blue Thunder and other colorful names which by government order had been translated into English because no one, except the Sioux, could pronounce the name in Lakota. Incredible that Americans could not pronounce Sioux words! The persons who translated the names were the "squaw men", white men who had married Indian wives and had learned the language. They were not well trained in English and were often forced to use their ingenuity in translating. On two different reservations the same Lakota words are translated as Crazy Bull and Holy Bull. The bull in this case being a buffalo. What it means in an enraged bull. It may be that the translator recalled something of the saying about crazy people being the spokesperson of God. The name of Chief Red Cloud of the Oglala Lakota tribe does not mean "cloud" but "meteor", the fiery, red flashing heavenly body that sweeps at times across the night sky. Lakota had a much smaller vocabulary than English. A cloud, a meteor or a comet were all something in the sky. At the time of his birth a meteor, a rare occurrence, passed through the skies.

The Commission brought this "signed" agreement back to Washington. All the X's had an Indian name written next to them. The Senate approved it as a Treaty of the United States. The Black Hills were lost to the Sioux, but as time went on they became known as the richest place on the face of the earth. While that is no longer true, it provided abundantly for the father of William Randolf Hearst of San Francisco, the newspaper magnet. His newspaper empire was founded on the fortune he inherited from the Black Hills. Lesser known persons shared in that wealth, but not the people they called the Sioux. In fact Shannon County which makes up most of the Pine Ridge Indian Reservation has in several recent studies been declared the poorest county in the United States. The people living on the Pine Ridge Indian Reservation have less money than anyone else in the United States, but many families outside South Dakota have in the American way realized a fortune from the gold in the Black Hills.

All these varied relationships have caused changes in the culture of the Lakota nation. In every culture there are elements that a tribe does not control but results from outside forces working independently of them and producing effects that will change the structure of their society. Before the white settlers moved among them, the Lakota people were a very wealthy nation. They had the resource of immense buffalo herds which, as we have noted, at that time produced wealth.

They proved to our age that a form of money was not necessary for wealth. With horses they became masterful horsemen. They could fight their own style of warfare and they could daringly hunt the mammoths of the plains, the buffalo.

With the buffalo they enriched their lives. Meat was almost always available. The number of items taken from the slain buffalos is incredible to us today. The list of items from food to clothing, from decorations to practical tools for daily life, from ornaments to garments and footwear, from tipis used as dwellings and council gatherings to carrying cases colored in the Lakota's bright geometric designs, from pillows stuffed with buffalo hair to games that used buffalo bones, from dried meat to raw tidbits fresh from the newly killed animal, the list totals over 100 items. The buffalo provided a supermarket of items for the Lakotas.

This great gift of nature combined with other factors to produce a culture of satisfying, human quality. Obviously much work was required to turn the buffalo into its many uses. Butchering the animal was a task of the women who would follow their men as they downed animals from the herd over acres of prairie or at the bottom of a buffalo kill where a stampeding herd ran off a cliff to their death.

The Lakotas hunted other animals and birds, but the buffalo was the prize animal of the hunt. Even in their dance they used hide and horns for decorating their elaborate dress. The constant work of the artists, and the Lakota are a tribe of artists, in decorating clothing and their tipi dwellings was remarkable. Of course, they used feathers from the eagle and plumes from other birds to enhance the design of their soft leather dress.

The horse which changed their life when it was introduced to their culture was another factor from outside that greatly enhanced their lives. They adapted so easily to riding swiftly across the plains, shooting arrows from almost every position, using their feet to hang on the side of the horse while shooting beneath his racing belly. The buffalo and the horse were gifts for which they thanked Wakan Takan (God) in their daily prayers.

The Lakota people had a solid spirituality that joined them in worship of the great mystery. It united them. Their were many shamans or medicine men, but all the religious leaders were liturgists who led them by the routine of rites and sometimes spectacular rituals to a steadiness in life and progress toward a life beyond. There was polygamy but a caring regard for the persons involved. Often a man's wives were blood sisters, already adjusted to working with one another.

The creative decoration of their dress and homes inspired a

great confidence in them. They were people of consequence. The fancy raiment of the men was among the most spectacular garb that men have ever worn. Even today in an organization like the American Indian Dance Theater, the native dress is raised to a spectacular height that the variety and technical advance of threads and fabrics makes possible.

A few years ago when money seemed to be more available, students from the Indian schools with instructors as chaperones would make trips to Europe to present exhibits of Indian dancing and meet with local groups dedicated to doing every thing in an Indian way. One weekend they met with a German group in a camp away from town for a thoroughly Indian celebration. Their tipis and dress were all hand made. The food was prepared in Indian style. Drums had been fashioned, and the fires lit. All were getting ready for the dance. When the Lakota students came out in their dress with chemically died feathers as decorations, a German boy of about five looked at the Indians and became speechless. He was struck by something in their appearance, but he could not enunciate the discrepancy he noted. Some adults tried to help him, and finally he put his thought into words. He knew that Indians used only natural feathers in their dress so he asked on seeing the bright orange, red, purple, blue, yellow and green feathers that modern chemicals had produced, "What kind of birds do they have in America?" The Indians had progressed more in their use of colored feathers than the German, in trying to maintain the ideal, state had allowed.

The exterior and interior decorations of their homes were works of art. The skins of buffalo that enwraps the tipi provided a perfect background for painting geometric designs or scenes of animals or buffalo hunts. Natural colors were drawn from herb or minerals in the soil. Sometimes liquids found in the bodies of slain animals were used effectively in producing various colors. Where in nature colors could be found, the Indians had found them. They were artists under the influence of the right hemisphere of the brain.

Within the tipi was an arrangement of soft buffalo robes that were placed around the expansive space within the conical shaped dwelling. Flaps at the top of the tipi could be arranged to allow

125

the smoke from the fire to escape into the outer air. But of greater interest was the dewlap around the lowest portion of the tipi's interior walls. The dewlap was made of tanned hides, or in later times cloth, that was arranged around the entire interior. It was attractive and functional. It provided insulation, but it also allowed for an artistic expression of the artists in the family. The designs were on a lesser scale than those on the exterior walls. The effect was a pleasing appearance that artistically distinguished one tipi from another. Since there was limited space, arrangements were made for every member of the family. The head of the household sat with his back to the dewlap and faced the entrance across the tipi. His wife or wives sat next to him and then the children were arraigned around the tipi walls. They would sit on the hides that covered the tipi floor. Normally there would be back rests, at least for the more important family members. Cooking would normally be done outside the tipi. For sleeping the family would stretch out with their feet toward the center of the tipi and cover themselves with the soft buffalo robes.

The furnished tipi was comfortable. It was a home of which the Indian family could be proud. It could be taken down in a short period of time and moved as a travois with the poles of the tipi dragging on the ground behind a horse. All the contents would be bundled and placed on the travois poles. The women of the tribe always struck and erected the tipi when the community moved.

The Indian man felt confident in this setting. He had the support of his family and community members. Women did not have a role of servants. Normally they did not speak at the tribal council, but they were not inferior. They were honored and when a warrior sought one out as a wife he would make a marriage gift for her hand consisting of a number of horses which would be left for her father. If the suitor was acceptable, the horses would be taken away and added to the family herd. Otherwise, they were left in place and the failed suitor would remove them.

Women were important and had work that was by tradition theirs. Everyone knew, and had known, for hundreds of years what was expected of him or her. Children grew up knowing that normally they must not cry lest by that sound their location be given away to enemy war parties.

It is interesting to note that a psychological method of discipline was used to maintain proper behavior among the children. When a child had done something deserving of discipline, the mother would act as though the child were not present. She knew where the child was but acted as though the child was not around her. She would talk to the other children but completely ignore the child who had misbehaved. She never hit the child but more effectively cut him or her from her attention. Normally the child after a time would recognize that he or she was being ignored. Then the child would run after her and anxiously grab her skirt. She would continue to ignore the child until she felt he or she had learned its lesson. If the child were older, he or she would be ostracized for a longer time. It is so important to be a recognized member of the group.

In this age when corporal punishment is not tolerated in the schools, it would be well for those responsible for rearing children to look at the very disciplined life that Indians lived. That does not mean that life was not enjoyable. It was. But all had to be done within the discipline that gave meaning to everything.

Indian children, it should be noted, were allowed to do almost anything they wished. They were free to roam. Boys played at hunting buffalo and would ride horses across the prairie free as the breeze. They would practice warfare and climb among the rocks of buttes near their tipis. Girls would gather together and play with dolls and practice being mistresses of their tipis. As the children advanced in age they would be involved in the work of men and women of the tribe. They had useful contributions to make.

In their play, children were free to do as they wanted as long as they observed the rules of avoiding betrayal of their location. The boys especially would be allowed to wander in groups and engage in what would strike modern parents as dangerous activities. They would climb trees and risk falling from them or climb over rocks where they might slip and fall. The underlying principle of their culture was to be prepared for any eventuality. In time their safety might require such climbing, and if they had practiced that from childhood they would be well prepared.

As horses came into their lives, boys were especially able to ride and learn the skills of an equestrian. The relationship of boys to horses was magnificent. They had dogs which were loved, but no animal took the place of the horse. As a fellow teacher once remarked, "If we could teach everything by an example from the horse, we couldn't fail." They would be so familiar with the animal that they would climb all over him and ride across the prairie in daring postures that increased familiarity but often ran the risk of falling. He might fall, he might hurt himself, but it was better to be a masterful horseman than never to try. Sometimes a bone would be broken and the young horseman would learn now to suffer without manifesting his pain. As he became a warrior, he would not show his enemies the suffering he endured. The children were not babied, they were prepared for life.

The broken bone would be set, and its healing take place over the following weeks. However, the child with the broken arm or leg would be anxious to return to the horse and ride away. This was bare back riding. Sometimes saddles were used, but for the most part boys rode in direct contact with the horses back and felt the energy exerted by the racing animal. Parents were controlled and did not manifest fear over the children's feat with a racing steed. They knew that they had to give him support and encourage his equestrian skills. He was growing up to be a warrior who would bring great pride to the tribe because of his skills in horsemanship and warfare. To experience danger in play would train him to dare when in combat he fought the enemy.

However, the settlers misunderstood the Lakotas when they came to settle the land around them. The Lakotas were a dominating people, a society confident in it itself with the structures of life that it had maintained for centuries. They were a warrior society.

The Europeans could not even pronounce their name. They called them Sioux.